P9-DET-760

Charles F. Kemp

D43
K32 p2
3dc

PREPARING
FOR THE
MINISTRY

THE BETHANY PRESS
ST. LOUIS, MISSOURI

© 1959

by

THE BETHANY PRESS

Library of Congress
Catalog Card Number: 59-10369

Printed in the United States of America

5 89
BPB

Lincoln Christian College

PREPARING
FOR THE
MINISTRY

CONTENTS

253
K32
c.2

DCHS
NASHVILLE

14 d

8 MAR 71

38695

PREFACE

Traditionally, the ministry has been looked upon as a "calling," and the author points out that it still is a calling. But a change has occurred in recent years. That change is illustrated most sharply in counselors' offices in schools and colleges where it has become commonplace for counselors to discuss with young people the choice of the ministry as a career, and the general educational preparation for the ministry. Planning one's education for the ministry and planning to enter the ministry hold great similarity to the planning for other professional services. Therefore, discussions of the ministry as a career have become part of the regular work of counselors in schools and colleges. In other words, planning for the ministry has become a matter of career planning rather than being placed in the realm of the dramatic.

Some young people who consider the ministry as a career are well suited for it. Some are not. It is as important to the ministry as to other professional careers that it be considered carefully by a young person and that the entry into the career result from both devotion *and* intelligent planning.

It is difficult to plan without information. The ministry has long needed a good source book that would provide the information that young persons who are considering this profession must have in order to look at and plan intelligently for a career in the ministry. This books fills the need.

The decision to enter a career must be based upon more than factual information about the career and upon more than factual information about one's abilities and potentialities. These are important but binding together both of these types of information are the complete personality, the individual, on the one hand, and the personality of a career on the other. It is *all* of a person that goes to work, not any small part. Any career has its own individuality. Therefore, a young person must look beyond the sheer facts. He must understand and feel himself, as a complete person, in a career that can provide the area of service for his particular individuality.

This book meets the need, too, for the background that goes beyond the usual enumeration of facts. One will be fully aware in its pages that there is more to a career decision than measured facts.

Preparing for the Ministry will be useful to young people who want to have greater insight into the ministry as a career. Counselors and others who work with young people will find that it is a valuable source book for use in counseling sessions. The author has included a section on careers related to the ministry that will enhance its use in counseling.

The author is a minister, educator, and professional guidance specialist. He is trained and experienced in all three areas. He has been highly successful and respected in each of these areas. His doctoral studies in guidance enriched his background of guidance experience. This richness has prepared Dr. Kemp to bring forth this needed and significant volume, *Preparing for the Ministry*.

ARTHUR A. HITCHCOCK
Executive Director
American Personnel and Guidance Association
Washington, D. C.

INTRODUCTION

This manual is prepared for young people who are considering the ministry as a life vocation. This includes a rather wide group. Some may simply be exploring the possibility along with several other possibilities. Some may be quite certain in their thinking that this is the thing they want to do but have made no definite plans. Some may already be committed to the ministry; some of them may have started their preparation and training.

Some will still be in high school, some in college, some may be through school and working, some will already be attending seminary. All of these groups have been kept in mind.

For this reason this manual is not designed as a book to be read straight through, although some young people may prefer to read it that way. It is a manual prepared to meet the needs of individuals at various stages of interest and preparation.

All have questions and problems at some time or other. Therefore, we have put the contents in the form of questions and answers. The questions have come from a variety of sources. (1) Many have come from young people themselves. They are the questions young people commonly ask, both in groups and in private conversation. (2) Some are questions suggested by pastors, theological professors, and church administrators. These are the questions they feel young people ought to ask but are likely to overlook. (3) Some are questions suggested by educational and professional counselors. These are questions they feel should be asked about any vocation if one is to make an intelligent and realistic vocational choice. We have attempted to bring together as many of these questions as possible.

Some of the questions will seem simple and the answers obvious. That is true for some people, but not for others. Some will be of interest to one group, some to another. All of them have been included because someone or some group felt they were important.

Some of the questions can be answered specifically and directly. Others have no easy answer. The way some questions would be answered would depend on the abilities, the personality, the background of the one asking the question. In such cases, we can speak only in terms of general principles. Some of the questions are controversial in nature. Different people would answer them in different ways. When this is the case, we have tried to be fair to the different points of view.

It is our purpose to provide information about the ministry and its preparation. That is what the vocational counselors call "occupational information." They place a great deal of importance on this matter; first, because the choice of a life vocation is such an important decision, and second, because one's choice of a vocation is determined largely by the information one has about it. Therefore, such a decision should be made only on the basis of information that is thorough, accurate, and complete.

We are not attempting to pressure or overpersuade anyone. It is our conviction that the ministry offers a great and challenging opportunity. We feel that through the ministry and the church one can serve the deepest and most vital needs of our day. This does not imply that everyone should become a minister. We do feel that everyone should live a life of service. We wish that everyone would serve the church in some capacity,

either as minister or layman. Everyone should not choose the
ministry as a vocation. Some people who read this manual will
not decide to enter the ministry. We hope the ideas presented
here will make them better-informed laymen. We hope this information will help them to co-operate with their minister in
the common task of Christian service that is shared by laymen
and clergy alike. A decision for the ministry should be made out
of a deep inner conviction that this is the thing one ought to do.
This manual is not meant to hurry or to pressure such a decision.
It is hoped it will provide the information that will make such a
decision realistic, informed, intelligent, and sincere.

Such a manual is not intended to take the place of either personal or vocational counseling; rather, it is a supplement to such
counseling. The young person who is considering the ministry
would do well to discuss the matter with his pastor, his school
counselor, or some trusted friend. It is hoped that these pages
will provide a background that will make such discussions more
profitable.

Although it has been prepared with young people in mind, we
hope it will be helpful also to those who work with youth—pastors, religious educators, sponsors of youth groups, school counselors, professional counselors, parents, and friends. We hope
it will provide an instrument that they can put into the hands
of the young people who come to them for guidance.

There is no order in which such questions occur that is common to all youth. We have grouped the questions into chapters
according to subjects. We have added an appendix, "On Learning How to Study," because it is our experience that this is extremely important at both the college and seminary level. For
some this could be the most practical section of the manual.
Many students are asking questions such as, "How can I make
the most of my time?" "How can I study more effectively?" We

are well aware that many more detailed discussions of study habits are available. We are also aware that seminary students do not know where to find them, or at least do not make the effort to do so.

We have also included in the appendix a list of the addresses of the national departments of the ministry of several of the major denominations and interdenominational agencies. A letter addressed to any of them will provide information about any particular group.

We would like to express our appreciation to the many young people and adults who have submitted questions and to the rather large group who have evaluated the answers. We want especially to express our appreciation to Jay Calhoun, National Director of Ministerial Services of the Disciples of Christ, whose encouragement and guidance in the preparation of these pages have been invaluable. Such a manual would have been impossible without the help of these people.

CHAPTER 1

Vocational Choice
and a
Decision for the Ministry

Why is so much stress laid on vocational choice?

The choice of a vocation is one of the most important and far-reaching decisions anyone ever makes. It is one of life's great "permanent choices." Like the choice of a life partner and the choice of a life philosophy, it affects all of a person's future. As one man said, "the choice of a vocation should be made carefully because it is a choice you will live with the rest of your life."

(1) The choice of a vocation is important because an individual's own happiness depends upon it. A man who enjoys his work, who goes to his task each day with enthusiasm and pleasure, is of all men most fortunate. On the other hand, the man who does not enjoy his work, who finds it monotonous, boring drudgery, has a problem that affects all the rest of his life.

Unfortunately, many do not enjoy their work. One study of 700 men found that over half of them wished they were doing something else. If they could have lived their lives over again, they said they would have chosen something else. This is most unfortunate.

President Eliot of Harvard said that he would gladly do for nothing what Harvard paid him for doing. He is a man who has made a good vocational choice.

(2) That vocational choice is important because a man's economic well-being and that of his family depend upon it goes without saying. Ours is a culture in which a mark of maturity is to be able to maintain one's self and one's family. The standard of living, the housing, the luxuries, education, and all related privileges are determined somewhat by the vocational choice one makes.

(3) Vocational choice is important because a man's contribution to society is determined by it. These are days of great needs —moral, spiritual, and social needs.

It has been said, "It is a tragic thing to live in an age and be unaware of its significance." Everyone's contribution is needed somewhere. A man's vocational choice determines what the nature of his contribution will be.

(4) Vocational choice is important basically because it is a spiritual matter. Religion is not something that takes place only on week ends. The way a man makes his living is a matter of spiritual significance. God has given us talents, abilities, aptitudes, and strengths. The way we use our time, our talents, and our strength is of concern to God himself. All this is included in vocational choice.

What is the basis for a wise vocational choice?

Counselors tell us that a wise vocational choice is based on two factors. The first is an understanding of the world of work. A person cannot make an intelligent choice of a vocation unless he understands what a person in this vocation does. He should have all the information about it that he can acquire. What are the duties and responsibilities of a person in this vocation? What is the nature of the work? What is the importance of the occupation? What is its future? The second is an understanding of one's self, his own abilities and aptitudes, his own likes and dislikes, his own strengths and limitations. Only as he understands himself, what he can do, what he wants to do, can he determine whether this is a field of work that he would enjoy, whether this is an area in which he could expect some measure of success, whether this is an area in which he would like to spend his time and his energy, whether this is an area where he will make his contribution to society and in which he would like to invest his life.

How does one decide for the ministry?

One decides for the ministry essentially the same way he decides for any other vocation—by finding out all he can about the ministry so that the decision is based on adequate, realistic information, and by making an honest evaluation of himself. He should ask himself some pointed questions: Do I have the ability to complete the training? Is this what I really want to do? Is there a need?

It is most important in deciding on the ministry (or any other vocation for that matter) that one seek self-understanding, thorough knowledge of the vocation, *and the guidance of God*. A decision should be made only after sincere and extended prayer. This does not eliminate the necessity of getting adequate information, helpful counsel and guidance, intelligent thought, but such a decision should always be made in a spirit of prayer and worship.

Where can I secure help in thinking through such a decision?

School counselors and guidance specialists can be very helpful. It is only fair to recognize that they are often not as familiar with the ministry as they are with other professions. Because of the difference in denominational requirements they do not have as much information about educational requirements and such matters as they would have for law, medicine, engineering, and some other professions. They can, however, be very helpful in administering and interpreting scholastic and vocational tests.

Pastors and theological professors are usually qualified to give guidance for preparation for the ministry. They are most familiar with the nature of the work, the educational qualifications, and other matters pertaining to such a decision.

Many denominations now have a guidance program that sponsors state or regional conferences in which such matters can be discussed. They also publish literature that will help in providing information. They will be glad to correspond with any young person seeking help on such a matter.

How or where can I secure information about the ministry?

(1) Take part in church activities, attend services and meetings. Whenever possible, go to youth conferences, camps, and conventions. Nothing can take the place of firsthand experience, sharing, and observing.

(2) Discuss the subject with your pastor. If you happen to be away from home, at school or working, write your pastor or find a pastor where you are. Ask him your questions. He will be glad to share his experiences. Find a pastor who is fairly successful and one who is happy in his work.

(3) Read. There are several good books on the ministry. The national office of almost every denomination and the National Council of Churches of Christ have some excellent pamphlet material you can receive by writing for it. These addresses are listed in Appendix II. Read the biographies and autobiographies of some of the great preachers like Phillips Brooks and Harry Emerson Fosdick. Read some of the good church histories to gain a sense of perspective on the church as a whole.

How long should it take me to reach a final decision about entering the ministry?

Several studies have been made to find out how long men have spent in reaching this decision. They reveal that the average candidate for the ministry has taken from two to three years to make the decision.

As with all averages, this means that some have taken more time, some less. Some never had any questions. This had always been the thing that they wanted to do. Some came to such a decision very quickly with little question or hesitation. Some have come to the decision after a long and extended period of time that may have involved considerable struggle.

The important question is not how long a period of time was spent, but were all factors considered? Is the final decision one that a person accepts? Does it represent a real commitment?

These figures remind us that vocational choice is a process. It involves gaining information about the vocation and an understanding of one's self. Sufficient time should be given to both.

CHAPTER 2

What Does It Mean
to Be
Called to the Ministry?

What is meant by a "call" to the ministry?

This has caused much confusion in some people's minds. It is not a term commonly associated with other vocations, although, as we shall see, it could be. One enters, selects, or decides on most vocations. We are told that we should be "called" to the ministry.

There have been many definitions or explanations of a "call to the ministry." They would include some common elements. The call comes from God. It is a call to meet a real need. It implies the ability to meet the need. As some people point out, there is a real sense in which the call of God is seen through the talents he has given us. It must be responded to by an act of complete commitment and dedication.

John Oliver Nelson, who has studied the question of the "call" probably as much as any one person, defines a call this way: "To be called of God is to be confronted with a life situation where

God is needed, and to realize that you must help meet the need."[1]

This definition recognizes that the call is from God; that it is to meet a definite need, and that it results in a feeling of compulsion or conviction on the part of the person.

Are all men called in the same way?

No. A call is always a personal matter. God calls no two people in the same way. The Apostle Paul had a very dramatic experience on the Damascus road. No such event is recorded in the life of Peter, James, John, Barnabas, or Timothy.

Read the lives of the great preachers—Phillips Brooks, Horace Bushnell, Washington Gladden, or Harry Emerson Fosdick. They all had different experiences; yet all were "called."

Are men called to other vocations as well as to the ministry?

Yes. According to the previous definition, the call is to meet a need—some may be needed as statesmen, some as scientists, some as teachers, some as doctors, some as social workers, and some as farmers.

In other words, God calls every man to a life of service. Some are called to service in the church vocations, but not all. When Sir William Osler gave up studying for the ministry in order to study medicine, that was no doubt the right thing for him to do. Medicine was his real calling, his vocation in the best sense of the term. According to the Christian faith and Christian teaching, God calls every man to a life of service. The church, the

---

[1]Nelson, "Protestant Religious Vocations," *Vocational Guidance Manual*, 1952, p. 28.

ministry, is one way a man can render a service. It is not, however, the only way. Any honest work that meets a need and that benefits mankind can be considered a "calling."

Is a call always a dramatic or emotional experience?

No. The majority of men could not point to some highly emotional, unusual experience. For many it was a gradual and a growing experience that resulted in a sense of commitment and dedication.

A little volume entitled *My Call to Preach* contains the stories of fifteen men who have achieved some success in the general area of church vocations. They all recorded their own experiences of a call. None heard an audible voice. None described anything spectacular. One spoke of a "slow maturing judgment"; another of a "deep inward conviction"; another of a "conviction that grew with the passing years." It was evident how frequently the word "conviction" appeared. Another said, "My call to preach is not a call which I can date. . . . Rather my call to the ministry has simply been a quiet conviction from which I have never known escape."[2]

This does not imply there is any lack of emotion. A conviction always carries emotion. It simply means a call need not necessarily be something that is sudden or dramatic.

What is the scriptural basis for a call?

The Bible is filled with illustrations of how men felt the call of God. In the Book of Genesis, there is the story of Abraham

---

[2]Edwin A. Hunter, comp., *My Call to Preach*. Tidings, 1946. (Methodist Church General Board of Evangelism.)

(Genesis 12:1-4) who was called of God to go to a new land. It is described in the Book of Hebrews, "By faith Abraham obeyed when he was called . . . and he went out, not knowing where he was to go." (Hebrews 11:8.) Moses was keeping the flocks of Jethro, his father-in-law, when he heard a voice from a burning bush that challenged him to go back to Egypt and face Pharaoh and demand the release of the children of Israel from bondage. A familiar story is the experience of the boy Samuel when he was living with Eli the priest. (1 Samuel 3:1-21.) Later Samuel was the instrument for calling David. (1 Samuel 16:11-13.) The first chapter of the Book of Jeremiah tells how he felt called of God and also how he resisted the call, feeling his own inadequacy. (Jeremiah 1:4-10.) Isaiah, chapter 6, contains one of the most detailed and dramatic of all descriptions of a call. It was in a time of national crisis and great need that young Isaiah went up to the temple and there he "saw the LORD . . . high and lifted up." Then in figurative language his experience reaches its culmination with the statement, "Whom shall I send, and who will go for us?" To this Isaiah responds, "Here I am! Send me." (Isaiah 6:1-8.)

The New Testament describes how Jesus called the disciples from the seashore (Mark 1:16-20, Matthew 4:18-22) and from a tax-collector's office. (Matthew 9:9.) Before he selected or called the twelve, he spent all night in prayer. (Mark 3:13-19, Luke 6:12-16.) The familiar story of Paul and the dramatic experience on the Damascus road is recorded in the Book of Acts. (Acts 9:1-12.)

It should be noted that all of these experiences were different. While some of these men had experiences that were dramatic and seemingly sudden, most of them had a previous period of pondering, wondering, and struggling with a situation. Even after the call the prophets and apostles had some moments of doubt and uncertainty. Although each resulted in a sense of commitment and dedication, they also needed a period of preparation and adjustment. For example, Paul went away for three years to ponder and think after his unusual experience on the Damascus road.

There are other passages in the Scriptures that are directly related to our lives. Over and over in the teachings of Jesus is a call to service, "He who is greatest among you shall be your servant" (Matthew 23:11; 20:27; Mark 10:44) and "'If any man would come after me, let him deny himself and take up his cross and follow me. For whoever would save his life will lose it; and whoever loses his life for my sake and the gospel's will save it.'" (Mark 8:34-35; also Matthew 10:39; 16:25; Luke 9:24; 17:33; John 12:25.)

The familiar parables of the good Samaritan (Luke 10:25-37) and the talents (Matthew 25:14-30) tell their own story. It is recognized that men have different qualities and abilities for "some should be apostles, some prophets, some evangelists, some pastors and teachers, for the equipment of the saints, for the work of the ministry, for building up the body of Christ . . . ." (Ephesians 4:11-12) And again, "Now there are varieties of gifts, but the same Spirit; and there are varieties of service, but the same Lord; and there are varieties of working, but it is the same God who inspires them all in every one." (1 Corinthians 12:4-7.)

What is meant by a "call" to the church?

A man is called not only to the ministry. There is a sense in which a church or a congregation shares in a call. This is what Richard Niebuhr calls an "ecclesiastical call."

He speaks of "(1) the *call to be a Christian,* which is variously described as the call to discipleship of Jesus Christ . . .; (2) *the secret call,* namely that inner persuasion or experience whereby a person feels himself directly summoned or invited by God to take up the work of the ministry; (3) *the providential call,* . . . which comes through the equipment of a person with the talents necessary for the exercise of the office and through the divine guidance of his life by all its circumstances; (4) *the ecclesiastical call,* that is, the summons and invitation extended to a man by some community or institution of the Church to engage in the work of the ministry."[1]

In other words it is through the call of the church that one finds and accepts the specific congregation where one expresses his ministry.

---

[1] *The Purpose of the Church and Its Ministry* by H. Richard Niebuhr. Copyright, 1956, by Harper & Brothers. Used by permission.

CHAPTER 3

The Ministry
and the
Church Vocations

What does the word "minister" mean?

The word "minister" in its original sense meant "service" or "one who serves." This is highly significant and puts great meaning into the word. In New Testament days it meant anyone who served.

(1) This is still true and, in this sense, everyone is a minister. This is one meaning of the Protestant principle of the "priesthood of all believers."

(2) Through the years, the word has come to be more specifically related to the ecclesiastical office; hence the use of the word "minister" today usually refers to one who serves as the pastor or minister of a church. It is often used interchangeably with the familiar words "pastor" and "preacher." These also have important meanings. The word "pastor" means a shepherd. The word "preacher" means one who proclaims a message.

(3) The term also includes other areas of service. Teachers of religion, administrators of state and national programs, mission-

aries, and religious educators are also ministers, so we speak of the ministry of teaching, the ministry of healing, the ministry of music, etc. In this sense there is a variety of ministries.

In whatever way the term is used, it ought not lose its original meaning. It should always include the idea "one who serves."

What do we mean by "church vocations"?

"Church vocations" is a broad general term that includes any vocation that is related to the church. We used to talk about the ministry, religious education, and the mission field as "full-time Christian service." This was a meaningful but misleading phrase. It was meaningful because it expressed the fact that it was a complete or full-time commitment to a life of service. It was misleading because it implied that these were the only forms of full-time Christian service, and this is not the case. The Christian doctor, teacher, lawyer, social worker, statesman, businessman, and housewife may all be giving full-time Christian service. All those who see their lifework as a calling, as an avenue of Christian service, all who dedicate themselves to the service of God and man through their vocations are giving themselves to full-time Christian service.

There are some who serve within the church. These vocations are known as church vocations. This term does not have the emotional appeal that the former phrase possessed, but it is a more fair and accurate description.

What are the church vocations?

Specialists in vocational guidance say that a person does not really understand any occupation unless he is familiar with the family of occupations of which it is a part. The ministry is one of a family of vocations commonly referred to as church vocations.

Pastoral Ministry. This refers to the functions of pastors of local churches. In larger churches it also includes associate and assistant pastorates. Where there is a large staff, the responsibilities may be divided, but, in the main, pastoral ministry includes all the responsibilities mentioned elsewhere in this manual: preaching, teaching, worship, counseling, stewardship, evangelism, promotion, administration—all the affairs related to a church and its congregation.

The pastoral ministry includes the largest number of persons of any of the church vocations. Much of this manual applies to the pastoral ministry.

World Mission. The story of Christian world missions includes some of the most outstanding and heroic names in history—David Livingstone, Adoniram Judson, William Carey, and, more recently, Wilfred Grenfell, Stanley Jones, and Albert Schweitzer. These names are representative of thousands of others, relatively unknown, who have served heroically and sacrificially in the far corners of the world. The missionary of today is carefully selected and highly trained. He has the usual theological training plus training in his area of specialization, such as medicine, education, evangelism, or agriculture, plus training in the language of the country in which he will serve. Thus highly trained and skilled, he is fighting disease, starvation, superstition, and ignorance all over the world. No more heroic or outstanding work is being done by anyone than by the Christian missionary.

One medical missionary summarized the motivation for missions in two sentences. "There is a certain satisfaction," he said, "in saving the life of a poor underprivileged sufferer who might die without the help you are able to give. There is a thrill in bringing the story of God's love to a darkened heart that might not have heard the story but for you."

American Missions. We no longer speak of foreign missions and home missions. Missions is ministering to human need wherever it exists. Some of these needs are in this country. There are missionary programs and institutions among the Indians of the Northwest, the Mexicans of the Southwest, the sharecroppers and migrants who follow the crops, the Puerto Ricans in New York's Harlem, the teeming thousands in the slums of Cleveland, Chicago, Los Angeles, and other great cities. Such projects require pastors, educators, administrators, nurses, social workers, secretaries—help of all kinds.

Religious or Christian Education. Jesus was known primarily as a teacher. The church has always been an educational institution. It deals with the most important education there is—an understanding of Christian truth and growth in Christian character. In recent years there has developed a new specialist among religious workers, the director of religious education, sometimes referred to as the minister of education. The training usually consists of a master of religious education or a B. D. degree with a major in religious education.

The majority of these directors serve on the staff of the local church, accepting the major responsibility for the educational program of the church, teaching and guiding children, young people, and adults in the Christian way of life. Many serve in the area, state, and national positions, directing the program of a denomination or an interdenominational council of churches.

Campus Ministry. John R. Mott once said that if he had his life to live over again, he would place himself near a great university, for there, among the students, was one of the greatest needs and greatest opportunities in the world. The minister to students attempts to meet this challenge. His work is done on or near a campus. Sometimes he is employed by the college or university to serve as a chaplain. Sometimes he is a university pastor representing a denomination who directs a student center for that denomination near a campus. He may also be called dean of the chapel, co-ordinator of religious activities, or director of religious life. In this case he serves all denominations represented on the campus. He directs a program of worship, fellowship, and discussion. He counsels with personal problems and, in general, represents the church on the campus.

Religious Higher Education. The church was the founder of higher education in this country. The first colleges and universities in America were all founded by the church. Even the state universities originally had clergymen for their presidents. There is a renewed interest in the place of religion in higher education today. Many men, drawn to religion as a vocation, enter the ministry of teaching. Most church-related colleges include a department of religion, or courses in biblical literature, or the psychology or philosophy of religion. Some state universities offer courses or have departments in religion in which a major in religion can be taken. In some states, there adjoins the campus a school of religion, conducted by the churches, in which students from the state university can take courses for which they receive credits which are recognized by the university.

Theological Education. The purpose of theological education is to train ministers to carry on the task of the church. It is graduate professional training.

The theological professor usually specializes in some major area, such as New Testament, Old Testament, church history, theology, preaching, or the pastoral ministry.

Military Chaplains. The work of the military chaplain is quite generally recognized. He conducts religious services for the men in the various branches of the armed services, does extensive counseling, helps to build morale, befriends and serves the men and women of the armed forces and their families in a variety of ways. Some men make a career of the military chaplaincy; others enter for a term of service and then return to the pastorate.

Requirements are the same as for ordination in a man's own denomination, plus special approval of one's denominational headquarters. After he is accepted for service, the minister has a short special course of training before entering active duty.

Institutional Chaplains. As a result of the pastoral psychology movement there has been a great interest in a religious ministry to the thousands in the various institutions in America. Pastors or chaplains have been added to the staffs of hospitals, mental hospitals, tuberculosis sanatoriums, prisons, reformatories, homes for retarded children, etc. This is a ministry that meets great personal needs. The people in the institutions cannot participate in a program of a local church. They need to worship; they need religious guidance, pastoral counseling, and pastoral care.

Preparation is the same as for the regular ministry, but in addition to or as a part of his preparation, the institutional chaplain should have some supervised or clinical training.

Church Administration and Promotion. American Protestantism is a highly organized, very complicated movement, consisting of many denominations, each one with a wide variety of state and national agencies and activities. In addition there are numerous state councils of churches and the National Council of Churches consisting of twenty-nine major denominations representing more than 30,000,000 members. These all require executives and administrative secretaries.

Space does not permit even listing the multitudinous activities that such groups sponsor, to say nothing of their significance. The work of Church World Service, as it ministers to the needs of the refugees, the homeless, and the starving around the world is but one example. It is a representative of the American churches.

Church Administrators. There are some churches that employ a business manager or a minister of administration who handles the business details of the church. These usually are large churches.

Religious Social Service. The church has always been concerned about the poor, the needy, the underprivileged, the dispossessed. Jesus, speaking of the hungry, the thirsty, the poor, the sick, the imprisoned, said, "'. . . as you did it to one of the least of these my brethren, you did it to me.'" For centuries the church was the source of most philanthropy and poor relief. It provided the background of modern social service.

Today there are countless social agencies—governmental and private—caring for the personal, social, and economic needs of the people. Some of these are under the auspices of the church.

Many people who prefer the field of social work as a life vocation serve in a church or a church-related agency. Some social workers prefer to serve on the staff of a local church, meeting the needs of people in some underprivileged or difficult area. Some serve on the staff of church-sponsored agencies, such as a settlement house, a mission in a slum area of a large city, among migrants, or in a multiracial community in New York or San Francisco.

Many denominations sponsor homes for children and homes for older people. Some groups have child welfare workers who are not related to a specific institution but serve a whole area.

Some people prefer group work and participation in character-building programs like the Y.M.C.A. or the Y.W.C.A.

Preparation for such positions varies with the field of work. In some cases a degree in social work is required. Sometimes, but not always, theological training is necessary.

Religious Journalism and Religious Publishing; Religious Radio and Television. The field of religious publishing is a large and influential one. It includes the whole field of religious journals, church school quarterlies and supplies, and religious books. Religious radio and television are relatively new. The church is still experimenting in the use of these media. It does not employ a large number of people full time as yet, but the number will undoubtedly increase in the future.

Sacred Music. Almost every church has some sort of musical or choral program. In the main this is on a part-time basis wherein the church utilizes as choir directors and organists the services of persons in the community who are musically trained. Some of the large churches do employ a full-time minister of music who usually directs a number of choirs and may, if trained to do so, carry some of the religious education program as well.

What is meant by multiple ministry?

Many churches are so large and their programs are so complex and varied that it would be impossible for one man to handle the work alone. In order to meet this need, an assistant or an associate minister or, in some cases, a staff of ministers is added. This is called a "multiple" ministry and the responsibilities are divided among the various ministers on the staff. Many churches have just two men, a pastor and an associate or assistant pastor. Some have a staff of specialists, such as a minister of education, a minister of stewardship, a minister of counseling, or other similar titles.

Should a person prepare for the ministry in general, or for one of the specialized areas?

In all vocational planning, it is considered best to get a general background of training for the total vocation first and then to specialize.

When a person is not sure which of the church vocations he wants to enter, but feels that he wants to serve in the church, he should start with the general preparation for the ministry. Later, he can move in any direction that he wishes and can take specialized training if he desires.

A person who is well qualified as to native ability could do well in several fields. It is best for him to have general training first. Opportunities may present themselves in more than one area during the course of his career, but a general background is always valuable.

A person who is definitely committed to one of the special fields, such as teaching in a theological school or serving as a chaplain, will benefit from having general A.B. and B.D. training and then gaining his special training in addition to this general background. He will be more effective if he understands the ministry as a whole.

CHAPTER 4

The Nature and Significance
of the
Pastoral Ministry

What is the nature of the task?

A person cannot make an intelligent choice of a vocation unless he knows what a person in that vocation does, how he uses his time, what tasks he will be performing five, six, or seven days a week. An individual cannot properly prepare for a vocation unless he knows what he will be doing in that vocation.

What does a minister do? What is the nature of his task? A minister has many different tasks and a wide variety of responsibilities:

(1) He is a *preacher*, first of all; that is, he has a message. He proclaims the gospel. This is the one thing he does that everyone knows about. Some people think that this is all he does. It is extremely important. Once or twice a week he will stand before his people and speak to them on the issues of life. As a preacher he will interpret the Christian faith, make the Bible real, condemn the evil in society, and support the good. As a preacher he will guide men into the Christian way of life, a way of service, hope, love.

(2) He is also a *pastor*. As a pastor he will go to people in time of need and in time of trouble. He will visit the sick, comfort the sorrowing, care for the aged and shut-in; he will make every effort to minister to every form of need. This is commonly referred to as pastoral care.

As a pastor people will come to him. They will come when they need help, when they are discouraged or confused or uncertain. Young people will come with their doubts and questions. Young couples will come to plan their marriages, older people will come when they have trouble in their homes and need help. People will come who have done wrong and are seeking forgiveness. People will bring him every form of human need and problem. This is called pastoral counseling.

Here the minister is dealing with real-life problems. Here he can make one of his most vital contributions, for when a person comes to him in trouble, the whole future of that individual "for better or worse" is in his hands.

(3) He is an *educator*—a religious educator. This is true even in those churches that provide a minister of education or a director of religious education. The pastor still is an educator and has a direct influence on the program of religious education. In the majority of churches, there is no one else on the staff and he supervises the educational program of the church. In a society like ours, where there is separation of church and state, this is the only religious training that many of these children, young people, and adults will receive.

(4) A minister has many responsibilities that are sometimes referred to as *priestly functions*. This would include officiating at weddings, funerals, and baptisms. It would include such all-important functions as leading the congregation in worship at regular Sunday services and on special occasions, such as at Christmas, Holy Week, and Thanksgiving. Some would feel that

to lead the people in prayer is perhaps the minister's most significant responsibility and highest privilege.

(5) He will also be an *administrator*. He will direct the program of the church, not alone to be sure, but he will be the one others look to and who is in the key position. This requires many activities, innumerable boards and committees. It involves budgets and fund-raising, or, as we would prefer, a program of stewardship. The church, in other words, is a group of people organized to accomplish certain purposes—the highest and most worth-while purposes within society. The minister is the head of that organization. In one sense, what the minister actually does is to help the church in its ministry.

(6) The minister is also a *scholar*. Preparation for preaching requires many hours of study. The minister is no longer the best-educated man in the community as he once was. In a university community he may have less formal training than some in his congregation. Nevertheless, the minister is the one who is expected to be an authority on matters of religion, and this requires constant reading and study. The minister must keep abreast of the latest thought in such fields as theology and biblical studies. He must be familiar with the latest findings in pastoral counseling and social ethics. He must know the thinking of the leaders in religious thought.

(7) As a pastor of a local church he is also the *representative of a denomination* or brotherhood. He works with other pastors in state and national programs. He serves on committees, attends conventions, teaches in youth conferences, helps support colleges and seminaries, and promotes missions. Our schools and missionary programs are dependent upon the interest the pastors create among the people in local churches.

He is also a part of a "larger church." This is sometimes called the "ecumenical church." This is the interdenominational, interracial, international program of the churches. It includes such projects as Church World Service and its program of rehabilitating refugees and feeding and clothing starving people everywhere. All these programs are dependent upon pastors in local churches.

(8) The minister is also a *community servant.* By virtue of his office, he will occupy a position of prestige and influence in the community. He will be asked to speak on numerous and varied occasions. His judgment and counsel will be sought on many public matters. He will be sought to serve on boards and committes of educational, social, and charitable institutions and agencies.

What is the significance of the pastoral ministry today?

When one considers all of the responsibilities that a minister is called upon to meet, he has a deep sense of the significance of the task. There is none greater. Let us, however, consider three major areas where a minister serves or where his influence is felt:

(1) A minister's task is significant because he serves an institution—the church. It has been the church which has kept Christianity alive through the centuries. It has been the church which has been the moral cement that has held society together. It has been the church which has created and nurtured other institutions, hospitals, schools, charities, and reforms. It has been the church which has created Christian character, Christian faith, and Christian personality in the lives of countless thousands. The minister's task is to make the church vital and real in our day.

(2) A minister's task is significant because his contribution is greatly needed in our world. The problems of the world are

moral and spiritual problems. We have had enormous advances in our scientific and technological developments. We are desperately in need of great advances in understanding, good will, justice, and love. The world is full of tension, intolerance, injustice, prejudice, hatred, and fear—the hope is in a moral and spiritual awakening. This is in the hands of the church and its leaders.

(3) The task of the minister is significant because he ministers to individuals. In the last analysis, it is persons that are important. The minister will have the opportunity of guiding youth in their spiritual growth, of helping people with every type of need and problem, and of ministering to many people as individuals, thus serving the church, serving the world, and serving persons in the name of Christ. This is the significance of the task.

What is the pastoral minister's relationship to other church vocations?

(1) The minister has a direct relationship with some church vocations. As a pastor of a local church, he may have a minister of education on his staff. He will certainly be working with area and national workers. He must know them and understand what they are attempting to accomplish.

(2) The minister must understand, interpret, and support the work of others—the work of the missions, of the church-related college, and of the seminary. All of these are dependent upon the financial support the minister can secure from the local congregation.

(3) In some of these related areas, the minister may serve on a part-time basis or as a volunteer. In a college or university town, he may need to act as a minister to students. In some com-

munities, he may be asked to serve as a part-time chaplain in a reformatory, a home for retarded children, or some other institution. He may have the chance to do some religious journalism by writing for religious journals or church school quarterlies or other publications.

(4) The minister may find that his work may lead to one of these areas of special emphasis. Denominational leaders and interdenominational leaders are usually selected from men in the pastorate. This is often true of professors in colleges and seminaries as well.

(5) The pastor will be called upon to serve as a counselor for those who are considering one of the church vocations as a life career. Young men and women who are considering the mission field, Christian education, religious radio, or any other area of religious work are likely to discuss it first of all with their own pastor. For this reason, he should be familiar with the whole range of church-vocations—the opportunities and the nature of the tasks. Only in this way can he render the fullest service to the young people who come to him.

What are the major misconceptions of the ministry?

There are many misunderstandings about the ministry as there are about other vocations. The two major misconceptions of the ministry probably have to do with the nature of the work and with the minister himself.

Many think of the ministry as a job in which a man preaches sermons. This is reflected in such clichés as "What a job! You have to work only one day a week." Many people, some who are active in the church, are totally unaware of the vast range of responsibilities and opportunities that demand the minister's time. We are speaking of the pastoral counseling, the calling, the administration, denominational and interdenominational programs, and other activities which we list elsewhere.

The other misconception has to do with the minister himself. Some think of him as a man interested only in religion, unaware of the realities of life about him. The fact is that a minister is not different from anyone else. He does have a deep conviction about the reality of religion and feels called to serve through the church, but he is interested in the same things, finds the same satisfactions and pleasures in life, as are common to all.

Some of these misconceptions are reflected in the movie industry, in certain novels, and in cartoons which caricature the minister as a long-faced, Casper Milquetoast type of individual who lives in a world apart. It should be noted that these misconceptions are gradually breaking down and people are coming to see the minister in a much more realistic light.

Is there one common purpose that runs through all of the different tasks and responsibilities?

Yes. The minister is a servant of God. Through all his various tasks the minister strives to serve God. He serves God by striving to meet the needs of the people and the needs of the world. The pastor deals with the deepest needs of life. All of these activities, all of these tasks have this in view—to make the Christian life and the Christian faith real in the lives of people, of men and women and boys and girls.

This is why he preaches sermons and goes to youth conferences, why he builds a building, raises a budget, meets with committees, sits down to counsel with persons, makes hospital calls, and performs all the other things a minister does. Buildings, committees, programs—all of these are means to an end, to make the Christian life and the Christian faith real in the lives of people.

CHAPTER 5

Personal and Educational Qualifications for the Ministry

What are the personal qualifications?

This is a difficult question to answer in a few words. There really is no adequate answer. It involves many things but certain qualifications should be emphasized.

Sincerity of character. This should be assumed. It does not mean one is expected to be perfect, for then there would be no ministers. It does mean one should be *sincere, trustworthy, and dependable.* A minister must be humble and have a character that is wholesome and clean.

Ability. Intelligence is not the determining factor in whether or not one can render a service. It does determine how much education he can acquire. There should be sufficient intellectual ability to complete college and seminary.

Emotional maturity. This is usually listed as one of the requirements for the ministry. It is a difficult term to define. In the main, it means the ability to act maturely, to make decisions, to accept a certain amount of disappointment and discouragement, to be reasonably free from stress and strain.

A love of people. Every minister must love people. He must be able to get along with people—all kinds of people. He must be able to work with people. He must have attitudes of patience, understanding, kindness, and love. This is the reason for entering the ministry—to help people.

A love of the church. A minister will serve in and through the church. He must believe in the church, enjoy work in the church, and have a deep confidence of the significance of the church and its mission. He must feel that this is where he wants to invest his life.

A growing Christian faith. The minister does not have all the answers. Quite to the contrary! But he does have a deep inner conviction as to the reality of the spiritual life and is making a sincere effort to grow in that direction.

A sense of commitment. J. Hudson Taylor went to China with the inner conviction that God was saying to him, "I am going to evangelize inland China and I will do it through you if you will walk with me." A person who enters the ministry should have something of this same sense of commitment to God and to the service of Christ.

He must have a willingness to work and a desire to serve. The ministry is a mission more than an occupation and one who enters it must have a spirit of dedication and commitment.

Does anyone have all of these qualifications?

No, not completely. These are ideals toward which we strive. No one has them completely. No one achieves them all at once.

It is somewhat reassuring to know that Phillips Brooks once failed as a teacher. He was so humiliated that he refused to see his friends. He didn't always have self-confidence—yet he became one of the greatest preachers this country has ever produced.

Horace Bushnell and Washington Gladden were men of faith—great faith—yet they both had an intense struggle with doubt. Gladden went through a period when he said his soul was "in great perplexity and trouble because it could not find God." Bushnell spoke of a time as a young man when he experienced "agonies of mental darkness concerning God."

Augustine the sinner became Augustine the Saint. Even the apostles fell far short of their intentions and often disappointed the Master.

The great preachers have not been men who had no faults or made no mistakes. They have been men who were conscious of their own weaknesses and were striving to develop those qualities of life and character that are worthy of this high calling.

Does a person have to be a leader to be a minister?

A lot depends on the definition we give to the word "leader." If we understand it to refer to the person who is always elected to office in high school or college, the answer is "No." Some such people enter the ministry, and this is good. However, not everyone must have a record of outstanding leadership to become a successful minister.

Some come into leadership slowly. They come into prominence later than others but they often last longer. There are many kinds of leadership. There is the kind that is popular, that is able to appeal to crowds, that commands attention and gets a following. There is also the kind that works behind the scenes, that depends on planning, persistence, and hard work. Both kinds are needed in the ministry.

It should be pointed out also that there are many ministries within the field of church vocations. Not all need to be in positions of prominence or directing groups.

Real leadership in any field grows out of conviction, intellectual capacity, understanding of others, persistence, the ability to continue in spite of discouragement and disappointment. It demands moral and spiritual strength.

What if my parents are opposed to my becoming a minister?

This is obviously a very personal and difficult problem. There is no single answer. Each case is different. Such a situation should be handled very carefully and after much thought and prayer. An understanding pastor can be a great help. Every effort should be made to help the parents understand your feeling and reasons for such a choice. The opposite is also true: you should make every effort to understand their feeling about the matter. Ultimately, the final choice must be your own choice, based on your own convictions and commitment. It is hoped that your parents will see the challenge and the value of it.

How much education is required?

Preparation for the pastoral ministry requires seven years: four years of college after which one receives an A.B. (Bachelor of Arts) degree, or its equivalent, and three years in seminary with a B.D. degree (Bachelor of Divinity). Specific areas of study will be discussed in the chapter on Theological Training.

For religious education the usual degree is an M.R.E. (Master of Religious Education). This varies from one to three years.

Some people who serve in the field of religious education take a B.D. degree, with a major in religious education.

For the mission field the training is varied, depending upon the type of mission work one plans to enter. Medical missions requires a regular M.D. degree, in addition to some training in theology, although the amount of training in theology will vary with different denominations. Some missionaries secure training in agriculture, public health, social work, nursing, education, or other areas. Most of this work requires at least a year of language training.

The ministry of teaching in either a college or seminary usually requires additional graduate study beyond the B.D. degree, such as a Ph.D. (Doctor of Philosophy) or a Th.D. (Doctor of Theology).

Why is so much education necessary?

The responsibilities of the ministry are so important and so varied that specific training demanding several years' preparation is felt to be necessary.

Ours is an educational age. The educated man is the accepted standard of our culture. As recently as fifty or sixty years ago, only ten per cent of the population went to high school, and only a very few went to college. In those days the minister was one of the few in the community who had a college degree. This is no longer the case. Today, almost everyone goes to high school and many go to college or to the university.

Ours is a generation in which extended academic preparation is required of anyone who would serve in one of the professions. There has been such a phenomenal growth in knowledge in recent years that standards of a previous generation are no longer adequate. The minister must be as adequately prepared as those in other professions. The lawyer studies seven years, the engineer at least five, the doctor nine or more, and the social worker at least five. The minister should be willing to secure preparation and training that is at least the equivalent in time and effort of that in these other professions. Seven years may well be considered the minimum, not the maximum.

When we discuss the content of theological training and point out the need for an understanding of the Scriptures, for a knowledge of church history and Christian thought, and for training in such practical matters as preaching, counseling, religious education and administration, it will be seen that there is scarcely enough time to include all the matters that are considered essential.

Have not some men been successful pastors without this much education?

Of course. Many pastors have trained themselves in the field. They have combined native ability with sincerity of purpose, hard work, extensive experience, wide reading, a love of people, and constant prayer and they have been very effective. Nothing that we can say here would minimize the value of what they have accomplished.

This fact, however, does not imply that one should limit his training. These men would be the first to advocate more and thorough education and training. Although a person can acquire skill by experience, proper training can decrease the time it takes to acquire the skills. Although information can be secured by oneself, it is seldom as complete and thorough as when it is acquired under the guidance of a skilled teacher, with the opportunity to share the discussion and the thinking of the students, and with adequate library facilities available.

In a former generation, successful lawyers, doctors, teachers, and social workers all had very limited training. All these areas recognize the need of more extended training today. The ministry is in a similar position. The real question is not how little training is necessary, but how complete a training can be obtained.

Isn't it possible to find schools where one can get all the training within four years?

Yes, there are many schools and Bible colleges that will provide in four years or less training that is considered complete. We are not speaking critically of them. They have a sincerity of purpose, an enthusiasm for the task, and a devotion to Scripture that is very valuable. It is the position of those educators who are associated with the American Association of Theological Schools, for example, that this is not enough. Ours is a generation which demands full liberal arts and seminary training.

It is also true that churches are more and more desirous of obtaining men with Bachelor of Divinity degrees. It should also be pointed out that difficulties often arise when a person wants to continue more advanced training and finds his credits from such schools are not acceptable.

How can one tell if he has the ability to complete college and seminary?

We are speaking here in terms of ability. Whether or not a person completes such a program depends on motivation and desire as well as an ability. The two best indicators are (1) grades and (2) intelligence tests.

(1) Grades are usually a good clue. A high grade average (that is, in the top 25% of one's class) is a good indication of the ability to complete further academic work successfully. A low grade average is a warning.

There are exceptions. Sometimes a person will receive poor grades because he hasn't tried, or doesn't care, or for some other reason hasn't utilized the ability he has. In this case grades would be deceiving.

Since teachers are human, and so are students, sometimes a person may get a low grade because of a poor relationship with a teacher. For this reason a grade average or group of grades is more accurate than a single grade, or the grades for one semester.

Whenever there is a question about grades as an indicator of ability, they should be checked with an intelligence test.

(2) The best single indicator of ability to do college or graduate work is a good intelligence test, properly administered. These are commonly called "scholastic aptitude tests."

Are mental or psychological tests of any help in determining a choice for the ministry?

Yes. Psychological tests are an accepted part of vocational guidance as conducted by schools, vocational counselors, the employment service, and industry. Some seminaries require them as a part of their entrance or qualifying examinations.

What are the tests that can be used?

There are literally thousands of tests. We cannot list them all. We will mention only the areas in which testing has been developed.

Intelligence tests. These are sometimes called I.Q. tests and are a measure of a person's intellectual ability. They are especially valuable in predicting academic success or failure.

There are both individual and group tests, verbal and non-verbal tests. The individual tests are much more accurate. Non-verbal, or performance, tests are used with those who have a language handicap.

Tests of Educational Skills. These are tests which are designed to measure the effectiveness of educational skills. They are tests of reading ability, inventories of study habits and such matters.

Achievement Tests. Achievement tests are designed to measure the results of the teaching process. They are standardized on large groups of people and measure the amount and accuracy of information one has acquired in certain areas. Some cover one specific subject like mathematics, English, or science. Some cover groups of subjects.

Aptitude Tests. Aptitude tests are based on the fact that people differ in the extent to which they possess the ability to develop certain skills. There are tests of aptitude in music, clerical work, mechanical ability, and such areas.

Interest Tests. Interest tests are designed to determine the areas in which an individual has fairly real and permanent interests. They are not a measure of aptitudes or ability. It has been found that people in particular occupations have roughly similar interests. It is then assumed that people who have the same patterns of interest will find satisfaction and be effective in the same field. An interest test tells the degree to which a person's interest compares with that of others already in the field.

Character and Personality Tests. Some of these tests are simple paper and pencil tests, some, like the projective tests, require training and skill to use. There is much discussion about the validity of such tests.

What are the chief values of psychological tests?

Perhaps the chief value, at least one of the major ones, is the fact that the test is objective in nature. Grades, letters of recommendation, and other sources of opinion are valuable but they are quite subjective. They are strongly influenced by personal likes and dislikes. They give one person's judgment and evaluation. A good test that is standardized on a large group of people and is uniformly scored whenever it is given provides a much more objective measure.

A good test enables a person's ability or characteristics to be seen in relationship to the general population, not just his own group or associates.

Tests assist in the making of realistic plans. Mental ability tests are very helpful in predicting the amount of academic success a person can anticipate or should expect. If there are limitations, it is best to know it and plan accordingly. If there are strengths, they should provide assurance and give confidence. They should be utilized and built upon.

Tests provide a kind of information that can be secured in no other way. A good test can tell if low grades are a result of a lack of ability or a lack of motivation or effort. A good vocational interest test will help in ascertaining whether a person has a genuine interest in a vocation or has been influenced by the glamor associated with it or by someone in it.

It should be pointed out that psychological tests should always be used by those who are trained to use them. They do have limitations which must be understood.

What are the limitations or dangers of psychological tests?

One of the big weaknesses of psychological tests is that many people put too much faith in them. They expect too much of them. The test experts constantly warn against such attitudes. They point out that they are not "magic" or "fortune-telling devices." They are clues that give information that cannot be secured in any other way, but they are not the only source of information. The test results should always be used with other information such as actual experience. No decision should be made on the basis of one test alone. When there is a question, there should always be a retesting or a rechecking of the results of one test by others.

Another danger is that of using poor tests or unqualified testers. There are literally thousands of tests. Some have not been standarized and have very little validity. A qualified, well-trained psychologist or educator is the person trained to know which tests are reliable. He also is the only one to administer and interpret such tests. Psychological tests are specialized instruments which require specific training. In such hands they are helpful—when used by amateurs, they may be harmful.

A person should be sure he has accurate information. Occasionally a person will say, "I think my I.Q. in the 8th grade was. . . ," or "my tests in the Army were. . . ." Often this is information he is remembering over a period of years. It may be extremely inaccurate. No decision should be made on anything but accurate, up-to-date information.

Another danger or warning is to recognize that each test is created for a specific purpose. An intelligence test is a measure of mental ability. It is not a measure of personality or motivation. It tells what a person can do, not what he will do. That depends on many factors an intelligence test can't measure.

An interest test is a measure of vocational interest. It tells whether or not the subject is interested in a field. It does not tell whether he has ability in that field. That must be determined by another test. A high interest may or may not mean he will succeed in this area.

Where can such tests be secured?

Public Schools. Most public schools have a routine testing program. This usually includes group intelligence tests, vocational interest tests, achievement tests, tests of educational skills such as reading, and sometimes personality inventories. When a school is large enough to have a guidance department or a school psychologist, it can administer individual tests in these areas.

Colleges and Universities. Most colleges and universities have a routine testing program as a part of their entrance requirements. If the school has a counseling service, there is usually one or more persons, depending on the size of the school, qualified to give tests to individuals. The psychology department of many schools will do testing for anyone within the school or out. For a person not enrolled in the university, there is usually a fee.

Psychologists, guidance centers, etc. A trained psychologist, whether in private practice or working in some agency, is usually qualified to administer such tests.

Seminaries and Theological Schools. Some seminaries are utilizing testing programs and have men on their faculties qualified in this area.

Employment Service. The United States Employment Service makes use of a battery of tests as an aid to vocational placement. These are vocationally oriented and designed for their own purposes and are not intended to be particularly suited for the ministry.

CHAPTER 6

Planning a College Program

What courses should one take in high school as a preparation for the ministry?

The primary consideration in high school is to take a college-preparatory course. It is very important to learn such basic skills as the use of the English language, how to read and write well. Although it is certainly a matter of secondary importance, some have found that the ability to type is a great saving of both time and expense.

How does one choose a college or university?

This is an important question because a person's formal or academic preparation for the ministry really begins with the selection of a college or university where he will receive his undergraduate training. It is a difficult question to answer because there is such a wide variety of schools and such a wide variety of tastes and preferences. What appeals to one may not appeal to another. Some prefer a large school and some prefer a small one. Some who live in a university town may prefer to stay at home, others may prefer to go away. These are individual matters, and each one must choose for himself in terms of his own likes and dislikes, and his own interests and opportunities.

Certain factors should be kept in mind. Before making the final decision, some definite questions should be asked.

Can you get the courses that you need? Does this school offer the courses that are considered necessary as a background for theological school? In other words, "Is this a school where the liberal arts are stressed?"

Is the school accredited? Being accredited means that it is recognized by a regional accrediting association. If it is, then its standing as a college will be universally recognized, and the student's courses will be accepted by any seminary. It also means that certain standards of excellence have been maintained.

This in no way casts a reflection on the quality of work done by some nonaccredited schools but it does issue a warning. A degree from a nonaccredited school is sometimes not accepted by a seminary or other graduate school. Much time is often lost in making up prerequisites or standardizing a degree.

What is the religious atmosphere of the campus? This includes more than whether or not courses in religion are taught. The religious atmosphere of a campus is a combination of many things—the history and tradition of the school, the attitudes of the administration, faculty, and student body, facilities and program for chapel and other observances, and the vitality of student religious programs. A student's religious life and experiences should grow as his academic and intellectual experiences grow.

What is the purpose of undergraduate education as a preparation for the ministry?

The best way to answer this question is to turn to the statement on "The Function of Preseminary Studies," prepared by the American Association of Theological Schools. It is a statement expressing the thought of a group engaged in theological training. It points out the definite practical results they hope will come out of college or preseminary studies.

Statement of Preseminary Studies

The Function of Preseminary Studies

College courses prior to theological seminary should provide the cultural and intellectual foundations essential to an effective theological education. They should issue in at least three broad kinds of attainment.

1. The college work of a preseminary student should result in the ability to use certain tools of the educated man:

   (a) The ability to write and speak English clearly and correctly. English composition should have this as a specific purpose, but this purpose should also be cultivated in all written work.
   (b) The ability to think clearly. In some persons this ability is cultivated through courses in philosophy or specifically in logic. In others, it is cultivated by the use of scientific method, or by dealing with critical problems in connection with literary and historical documents.
   (c) The ability to read at least one foreign language and in some circumstances more than one.

2. The college work of a preseminary student should result in increased understanding of the world in which he lives:

(a) The world of men and ideas. This includes knowledge of English literature, philosophy, and psychology.

(b) The world of nature. This is provided by knowledge of the natural sciences, including laboratory work.

(c) The world of human affairs. This is aided by knowledge of history and the social sciences.

3. The college work of a preseminary student should result in a sense of achievement:

(a) The degree of his mastery of his field of study is more important than the credits and grades which he accumulates.

(b) The sense of achievement may be encouraged through academic concentration, or through "honors" work, or through other plans for increasingly independent work with as much initiative on the student's part as he is able to use with profit.

What is the content of pretheological education? What specific courses should one take in college in preparation for the ministry?

These are essentially the same question. Both deal with the problem of what specific areas or courses one should select out of a college catalog. Again, the American Association of Theological Schools has prepared a statement to guide pretheological students:

SUBJECTS IN PRESEMINARY STUDY

The following is regarded by the Association as a minimum list of fields with which it is desirable that a student should have acquaintance before beginning study in seminary. These fields of study are selected because of the probability that they will lead in the direction of such results as have been indicated.

It is desirable that the student's work in these fields of study should be evaluated on the basis of his mastery of these fields rather than in terms of semester hours or credits. That this recommendation may help the student faced with the practical problem of selecting courses, however, it is suggested that he take 30 semesters or 90 semester hours or approximately three-fourths of his college work in the following specific areas:

English—literature, composition, speech and related studies. At least 6 semesters.

History—ancient, modern European, and American. At least 3 semesters.

Philosophy—orientation in history, content, and method. At least 3 semesters.

Natural sciences—preferably physics, chemistry, and biology. At least 2 semesters.

Social sciences—psychology, sociology, economics, political science, and education. At least 6 semesters, including at least 1 semester of psychology.

Foreign language—one or more of the following linguistic avenues to man's thoughts and tools of scholarly research: Latin, Greek, Hebrew, German, French. Students who anticipate postgraduate studies are urged to undertake these disciplines early in their training as opportunity offers. At least 4 semesters.

Religion—a thorough knowledge of the content of the Bible is indispensable, together with an introduction to the major religious traditions and theological problems in the context of the principal aspects of human culture outlined above. The preseminary student may well seek counsel of the seminary of his choice in order most profitably to use the resources of his college. At least 3 semesters.

Of the various possible areas of concentration, where areas of concentration are required, English, philosophy, and history are regarded as the most desirable.

THE NATURE OF THIS RECOMMENDATION

The Association wishes to point out two characteristics of the list of preseminary studies it is recommending:

First, this is a statement in minimum terms. We make no attempt to list all the work which it would be profitable for a student to do. It is thus possible to include many other elements in one's college courses, while still working in what the Association regards as the first essentials.

Second, the emphasis is on a "liberal arts" program because, in the judgment of the Association, the essential foundations for a minister's later professional studies lie in a broad and comprehensive college education.

What do all these courses (as recommended by the AATS) have to do with preparing a person for the ministry?

Preseminary studies are designed to produce certain results, results that will have a direct bearing on how effective he is as a pastor and as a preacher. At times it does seem that some of his assignments and some of the books he has to read are not closely related to the work of a pastor in a church. When we consider the undergraduate progam as a whole, however, it can be seen as a definite and practical background for his future services.

The minister must be able to express himself. He is largely dependent upon his use of language, so English is indispensable. He also should be familiar with at least some of the great literature that is a part of our heritage and culture. He must understand life and this deals with life.

We cannot understand the present unless we have a knowledge of the past—hence history is an essential in a minister's
background.

The minister deals with ideas and values; therefore he needs
courses in logic and philosophy. He lives in a world of science.
The minister, while not a scientist in one sense, certainly must
have a knowledge of the scientific world and some appreciation
of the scientific method.

The minister, and his church, will be a part of society. He will
be working with groups and be subject to social pressures and
influences, and as a result, it is important that he is acquainted
with the whole field of the social sciences—sociology, economics,
and political sciences.

He will be working with people. In fact, this will be his major
concern; therefore, psychology, which is a study of human behavior, is a necessity.

An appreciation of other people and their culture is valuable,
so a foreign language is recommended.

The seminary will provide the more advanced training in religion, yet the ministerial candidate needs a knowledge of the
Bible and the place of religion as a part of our culture and
heritage. Some religion courses are recommended to parallel his
other undergraduate preparation.

What should a person select as a major in college?

While a person is in college, he must select a major field of
emphasis. This usually means that about 25% of his course work
will be in this field. Obviously it should be in an area where a
person has a major interest. No one wants to spend that much

time and effort unless it is in a field that he enjoys and in which he finds satisfaction.

It also may be determined somewhat by the school he attends. Some schools have a much stronger department in some fields than in others. Sometimes an individual professor may make a difference. A student might be attracted to history as a major in one school because the professor is a man who makes history challenging and vital. These are matters that are well to investigate before selecting a school.

Basically, the decision should be made in terms of "what will be the most helpful in one's future training and experience."

Should a person major in religion in college?

There are two schools of thought on this matter and both have good arguments in their favor.

Some would say that for a person going into the ministry his greatest need is for a knowledge of religion and therefore religion should be his major. There is much to be said for this point of view. One cannot have too much information about religion.

It is important to issue a warning at this point. When religion is selected as a major, the student must be very careful to include all the other areas mentioned in the AATS suggestions in his program. He still needs a broad liberal arts background.

The temptation is for a student because of his religious interest and motivation to "load up" in religious courses. When this is done, two unfortunate results can occur. First, he may not have enough prerequisites to enter seminary and find he loses time in making up deficiencies. More important, he needs these other courses for a well-rounded background.

There are those who would advise against a major in religion. Their position is that a liberal education is so important that this is all that can be accomplished in four years. Too narrow a concentration in religion does not leave time for the general background that is needed. They also point out that there are often large areas of duplication. For this reason, they feel concentration in religion should be left to the seminary. This does not mean that one should not take any religion courses. On the contrary, if his major is another field, it would be valuable for him to take electives in religion.

The important thing to remember is to keep a balance: the one who majors in religion should be sure he has the courses which will give him an understanding of the arts and sciences; the one who majors in another discipline should have some introduction and understanding of religion.

What are the advantages of a church-related college?

A church-related college or university is an institution of higher learning that is in some way directly related to a religious body, denomination, brotherhood, or fellowship. In most cases, it was founded by the leaders of the church for the purposes of providing higher education.

The church-related school is maintained and supported, at least in part, by the contributions of the churches or church, as the case may be. Administratively, it means that pastors and church leaders are in places of influence on boards and committees and in offices of importance.

In terms of curriculum and teaching staff, it means that the Christian faith and the Christian heritage are recognized and accepted as a part of the total educational picture.

For these reasons many people recommend a church-related college for the ministerial candidate. Its curriculum is usually designed with the pretheological student in mind. It relates him to his own denomination or fellowship. The church-related college can provide good personal guidance for the pretheological student in academic and personal matters that are related to the ministry. It usually has a religious atmosphere and a spiritual emphasis. While providing complete academic freedom, it attempts to see all of life from a Christian perspective and enables the student to grow in his religious development and understanding as he grows in his intellectual and academic experience.

Can a pretheological student get adequate undergraduate work at a state university?

Many pretheological students receive their training in state universities. Many students decide to enter the ministry while attending state universities. There is a great deal of difference in universities. What applies to one may not to another. There is no reason why one cannot get pretheological training at a state university providing the liberal arts are stressed.

One cannot usually major in religion at a state university although there are some exceptions. Several schools have a school of religion or a Bible Chair adjoining a campus where one can take courses in religion that are accepted for credit toward a degree in the state university.

How much does the education cost?

This is a common question to which there is no one answer. There is a great deal of difference in tuition costs, housing, etc. Then, too, the charges vary from year to year as costs change to meet current prices. The best procedure is to write to the school of your choice to get firsthand information as to actual expenses. If you have no choice, you can write to several schools for such information.

Can a person earn a part of or all of his education?

Yes. Many students go to school with limited funds. Some work part of their way, and some all of their way through school.

Any college or university will provide information about scholarship and loan funds, and will help find on-campus or off-campus jobs. The U.S. Employment Service will help in locating part-time work. Summer jobs can help provide funds for the year.

It should be pointed out that many factors besides tuition determine a person's total expense. Clothing, housing, whether or not a person belongs to a fraternity, how much he spends on entertainment and social activities—all of these determine the total expense. These are individual matters and each person must determine them for himself.

Does part-time work interfere with one's education?

This depends. Some do allow employment to become so time-consuming or so tiring that there is not sufficient time or energy left to study. Some priorities have to be established. A person must plan a program that includes both employment and class and study time. Sometimes it is necessary to extend one's education over a longer period of time. Sometimes a loan is better than a job that consumes too much time. Sometimes assistantships and fellowships can be secured that combine study and employment.

What is meant by a ministerial scholarship?

Many colleges (especially church-related colleges) provide scholarships for pretheological students. These scholarships vary from one-half to full tuition.

Some local churches have scholarship aid available for young people in their congregations who study for the ministry.

Do people ever change to the ministry after they have begun preparation in another field?

Yes, many do. Every seminary has students who began preparation in business, education, medicine, music, engineering, or other fields. Some had completed their training in another field before they decided to enter the ministry.

What should I do if I have already started preparation in another field?

This is not at all uncommon. If you have been studying agriculture, engineering, education, or anything else, and decide definitely that you wish to enter the ministry, you would do well to evaluate your whole educational program and begin to secure the prerequisites for theological school as soon as possible.

Your training thus far has value—even for the ministry. Anything that helps you understand life, people, and the world can be used to advantage. But you should secure as many of the courses suggested for pretheological education as you can.

Not every seminary requires that deficiencies be made up, but some of them do. The sooner you can secure an A.B. degree, or its equivalent, the better. Without it, much time may be lost in making up deficiencies in order to be accepted by the seminary.

If you are in a situation such as is described by the question, you would do well to contact the seminary of your choice, send them a transcript of your credits thus far for evaluation in terms of what would still be needed to be accepted by the seminary. This could save much time and expense.

Is it important to take part in church activities while in college and seminary?

Yes. Anyone planning to enter the ministry should take advantage of every opportunity to work in the church, the church school, youth groups, and in other activities of the church for several reasons.

(1) It helps a person understand and evaluate his own strengths and interests. Vocational counselors speak of the value of "tryout experiences." George E. Myers, in his book, *Principles and Techniques of Vocational Guidance,* says, "One who samples the fundamental experiences of an occupation knows more about his aptitudes and limitations with reference to that occupation and sometimes reference to an entire group of related occupations, than he could possibly learn in any other way."[1] The church is in a unique position in this regard. There are many opportunities for experience within the church before one enters it as a full-time vocation.

(2) Participation in church activities has an educational value. Books on religious education are helpful but they are no substitute for teaching a class of children. Those who have had first-hand experience in the church profit most from their theoretical training. Those who have worked as laymen in a church program will be better equipped to work with laymen as pastors.

---

[1]By permission from *Principles and Techniques of Vocational Guidance,* by George E. Myers. Copyright, 1941. McGraw-Hill Book Company, Inc.

(3) Basically one should participate in the church for the same reason everyone else does. Here is a need and here is a service he can render.

Doesn't college sometimes destroy a person's religious life?

It is commonly recognized that religious problems are often accentuated on a college campus. Some students are faced with the necessity of completely re-orienting their thinking. In many cases this may be the student's first contact with points of view other than his own. It may be the first time that he has heard the position of his home church or of his parents challenged or debated. It may be further complicated by the fact that many students come to the campus with very limited religious background and training. Here he must relate his religious belief to all the findings of history, philosophy, psychology, anthropology, science, sociology, and the rest of the curriculum. This is not easy.

It is also only fair to recognize that the prevailing atmosphere of higher education in America is predominantly secular. Some schools, some departments, and some professors are indifferent to religion; some ridicule traditional beliefs and practices; some are antireligious.

When a preministerial student participates in a class in which religion is treated critically or minimized, it may cause some difficulty and even some embarrassment in his own thinking. Such experiences can be difficult for any student but for the ministerial student, it means his whole vocational commitment, his life plans and dedication are involved.

Such students should remember that this is no unique experience. Everyone has faced it. Some of it is good. While we would see no reason why a student needs to expose himself to continuous antireligious influences, neither do we feel that he should be shielded and protected. It is only as he can face the encounter of religion with other fields of learning that his religion becomes real. Furthermore, this is the world in which a pastor's people will live. These are the problems the youth in his church will face. Only as he has faced such questions himself can he help others who are confronted with the same problems.

If at times it seems confusing and perplexing, he should feel free to talk it over with a wise pastor, an understanding professor, or a university chaplain or minister to students. Such men are glad to help.

In the long run, it is hoped that a college education will deepen and not weaken a person's religious faith.

How can one utilize his summers to broaden his education and experiences?

Youth camps and *conferences* are extremely valuable. They provide a program of worship, fellowship, recreation, instruction, inspiration, and guidance. That is one of the most effective programs the church has found for youth. They usually provide good leadership and are held in a setting that makes use of the beauty of nature or the facilities of a campus. Every person considering one of the church vocations should take advantage of the opportunity to attend at least one summer camp or conference.

Youth caravans and *work camps* provide both an educational experience and a chance to render a real contribution at the same time. Youth caravans consist of a group of young people who travel throughout the summer going to several different churches. They conduct services, speak to youth groups, help conduct such projects as vacation Bible schools and youth activities. A work camp consists of a group of young people who carry out a service project under the direction of a qualified leader. The campers may repaint a rural church, set up a playground or do any one of a number of things that need to be done that would not otherwise get done. Some of these work camps are overseas. In these experiences young people receive a broad background of experience. They widen their circles of friendship, gain an understanding of human needs, and have the satisfaction of rendering a real service to a church or community.

Does a personal study of the scripture provide a background for seminary?

Yes. One of the big handicaps professors in theological schools encounter is a limited knowledge of biblical content on the part of the students. A seminary does not have the time to teach content and technical interpretation and understanding. A knowledge of the content of the Scriptures is something a person can and probably should secure for himself.

A person who is planning to enter the ministry should have some regular plan for reading the Scriptures. Ten minutes a day over a period of time can make a real difference.

CHAPTER 7

Making the Most
of
Theological Training

What is a theological school?

Dr. Niebuhr, in his very significant book entitled *The Purpose of the Church and Its Ministry,* defines a theological school as *"the intellectual center of the church's life."*

From the standpoint of the candidate for the ministry, the theological school is the place where he receives his professional training. Undergraduate school is where he secures the background necessary for anyone in the ministry. Theological school is where he secures the advanced training in religious knowledge and the skills and techniques that are necessary to render his fullest service.

What is the difference between a seminary, a divinity school, and a theological school?

There is no difference. The three terms are used interchangeably. Some schools have other titles such as "College of the

Bible" or "School of Theology" or "School of Religion." The basic question is, "Does it offer a B.D. degree?"

What is the purpose of the theological school?

To refer again to Dr. Niebuhr, the ultimate purpose of both the church and the seminary is to increase the love of God and love of neighbor among men. All of the courses of biblical studies, theology, church history, Christian ethics and all the procedures and skills of homiletics, worship, missions, religious education, counseling, and church administration are dedicated to this end.

The purpose of the theological school is to prepare a person with sufficient understanding of the reality of the Christian faith and heritage and sufficient skills in dealing with people through preaching, teaching, counseling, and group activities to render a real service to individuals, to the church, and to society in the name of Christ.

How many theological schools are there?

This is difficult to answer because there are so many schools in the country that offer training in religion. Some of them are Bible institutes, some are four-year colleges, and some are fully accredited graduate schools of religion. It would be very difficult to find a list that included all of these schools.

The American Association of Theological Schools is an organization of graduate schools of theology that have set up certain standards for acceptance or accreditation. These standards include such things as the competence of the faculty, entrance requirements, adequacy of library and other facilities. The association has two categories of membership: "accredited" and "associate" members. The latter do not fill quite all of the requirements for full accreditation. These classifications vary from year to year, but at present 82 schools are accredited and 30 some are listed as associate members. A letter to the national headquarters of any denomination will give information about the schools sponsored by that church.

How does one select a seminary?

This is a difficult question to answer because there are so many factors involved. For some it may be no problem. They are assigned to a seminary and that eliminates the question. All we can do is point out certain elements that should be considered.

(1) *Faculty.* No seminary is stronger than its faculty. Education is received from men not buildings. Is the faculty well trained, qualified, and committed?

(2) *Facilities.* The library is the most important of all for educational purposes, but the buildings, the surroundings, and the setting all have an influence.

(3) *Denominational or interdenominational affiliation.* Some will prefer a school with a denominational affiliation. This has real values: it presents a student with a point of view that will be common to his ministry; it relates him to an alumni group with which he will be associated throughout his career. Some will prefer a nondenominational or interdenominational background because of its larger faculty and ecumenical approach.

(4) *Opportunities for field work and experience.* Some may need such an outlet for economic reasons. All need field work experience for practical training experience. One should know what opportunities are provided.

(5) *Theological position and outlook.* There are many theological points of view in the religious world. One should know before selecting a seminary the view or position of the school where he will receive his major training.

(6) *Accreditation.* Membership in the American Association of Theological Schools gives a certain amount of prestige and is a guarantee of having credits accepted if one desires to go into further graduate training.

(7) *Spiritual climate and atmosphere of the seminary.* This can be very important. Does the school, faculty, and student body alike have a spirit of reverence, devotion, and commitment to the Christian faith and the Christian cause?

(8) *Location.* The location of the seminary can have a real influence on the opportunities one may have when his education is completed. If one wants to serve in the East, the Middle West, or the Far West, for example, he might want to choose a seminary in that location. However, this is not always so; some who attend school in the East serve in the Middle West or Far West; in fact, many do. It simply is another factor to be considered.

What grades are required for seminary entrance?

This varies with the seminaries. Some schools simply require an A.B. degree or its equivalent. Others require a certain grade average. A catalog of the seminary or a letter to the seminary dean or registrar will furnish such information.

How does one finance a theological education?

There is no one answer to this question. A person who is concerned about the financial arrangements for his theological training should investigate such areas as the following:

Tuition and scholarships. Tuition and fees vary with different schools, so one should get accurate information from the schools in which he is interested. Many schools have a good scholarship program. The ministerial student has an advantage at this point over most other forms of professional education.

Housing. One of the major areas of expense is housing, especially for the married students. Many schools provide low-cost housing, usually in the form of apartments for married students and dormitories for single students.

Student pastorates, assistant pastorates, directorates of religious education, and youth work. Most theological students are engaged in some form of field work that provides an income. The amount varies greatly. Student pastorates frequently include a parsonage.

Part-time work. Some schools use students as secretaries, and in campus maintenance and yard work. Some students find employment in the community.

Loan funds. Many schools provide loan funds that are available to students who need financial assistance.

Church scholarships. Some local churches sponsor a student who is preparing for one of the church vocations.

The catalogue of the seminary will carry information about such items as these. A letter to the seminary will answer any specific question.

What kind of men will I be associated with in theological school?

We assume this question means, "What kind of students will I be associated or living with?" These students are the same as students anywhere. There is no type that can be called a typical theological student, as all expressions of personality can be found in the classes of a seminary. In the main they can be described as a very high-minded, sincere group of men who are dedicated to service in the church.

If the question means, "What kind of men make up the faculty?" the answer is the same—all kinds. The men who comprise the faculty of a theological school are men who have specialized in some area of theological study. Some have distinguished themselves as pastors before becoming professors.

What does a person study in seminary?

Different seminaries divide their curricula under different headings, but most of them include those which are necessary to produce a competent, fully trained minister.

A knowledge of both Old and New Testament Scripture is absolutely basic, so courses in *biblical studies* are included. The minister must also be fully aware of the Christian heritage, the development and growth of the church and its influence. Since we understand anything only as we see it in the light of its history, courses in *church history* are a part of the curriculum.

The minister must both understand and interpret the Christian faith and the Christian life, so courses in *theology* and *Christian ethics* are an essential part of the program. The minister must be proficient in certain skills. Since he has a major responsibility for preaching, he must have courses in *homiletics* or the *art of preaching.*

Since he is also an educator and often supervises the program of education, he will take some courses in *religious education.* Every preacher is also a pastor, so he is trained in the field of *pastoral counseling* and *pastoral care.* Since he directs the program of a church, he will have courses in *church administration.*

Each of these fields is an area in which men have spent a life-time of study and research. The specialists in the field are the first to admit that their knowledge is far from complete. This only emphasizes the importance of the seminary years. In a comparatively brief time, the theological student must get a working knowledge of each of these areas, and integrate them into a whole so that he can minister effectively to the needs of his people.

What is meant by "content" and "applied" courses?

Content courses are courses that include a body of truth or information. Applied courses are courses that have to do with the practical functions of the ministry. Examples of the former are biblical studies, theology, and church history. Examples of the latter are homiletics (or the art of preaching), counseling, religious education, and church administration.

What is the relationship between the content and the applied courses?

They are two parts of the same whole. One strengthens and supports the other. The lack of one weakens and handicaps the other. For example, preaching is one of the minister's major responsibilities. If a man is to preach effectively he has to have a message. This means he must have an understanding of Scripture, theology, and the Christian faith. However, he must also be able to organize his material and present it in such a way that his hearers will understand and will be convinced of the reality of what he says. If a man has good thoughts but a poor delivery, his message may not get to the people at all. If he has a good delivery but does not understand his message, it is merely a presentation or a show; in other words, an effective preacher must master both content and applied courses.

The truth of the matter is that there are elements of both in every course. A course in "content" has many practical implications. A course in methods and techniques, whether it is in counseling, preaching, or religious education, has definite relationships to the biblical, historical, and theological fields.

What is meant by "field work"?

In most theological schools students are engaged in some form of part-time work in a church or some other institution. The most common practice is for the student to secure, or to be assigned to, a student church (sometimes called a student pastorate) which he serves on a part-time basis. This usually consists of conducting services on Sunday and doing whatever else he can do in the way of calling and youth work. Some students live on the field, when a parsonage is furnished, and drive to and from school. Some students live on the campus and go to their churches on the week ends.

Some students serve as assistant pastors in large churches. Some serve as directors of religious education; some may serve as sponsors of youth groups or teachers of church school classes.

An increasing number of seminaries require a year's internship. In this arrangement a student is placed in a church full time for an entire year. This usually is done between his middle and senior years in seminary. Under this arrangement he gives a full year to gaining practical experience before returning to the seminary to complete his academic work.

Should field work be considered a learning experience or a service rendered?

It is both. The theological student must have a twofold approach to field work. He should utilize his field-work experience as a source of learning which gives meaning to his theoretical studies. It is training of a very helpful and practical sort.

He should also remember that it is a service. If he has a student pastorate, his is the only preaching, the only pastoral services that these people will have. This church, small though it be, is their church just as much as any large, beautiful city church with a huge staff. If he teaches a church school class or serves as the sponsor of a youth group, his is the only training these young people will have. When he makes a hospital call or counsels with a teen-ager, this is the only pastoral service these people will receive. In this respect, he is not doing field work—he is the pastor.

What are the values of field work for the theological student?

Field work is a real learning experience. The student has actual experience in such areas as preaching, pastoral calling, and church administration. It gives a note of reality to his classroom experience.

Field work has a further value in giving the student an opportunity to render a service at the same time he is completing his education. This can be a real factor to some older students who feel they have been going to school "all of their lives." It enables them to feel they are also making some contribution and gaining some experience.

For some, especially the married students, it can fill a real economic need.

The value of field work educationally depends to a large extent on the amount of supervision provided by the seminary.

What are some of the dangers of field work?

A student may be thrust into a difficult situation before he has adequate training and experience to cope with it. This is of no benefit to the church, the people involved, or the student.

Field work can result in a divided interest so that the student either neglects his church work for his studies, or neglects his studies for the church work, with the result that neither is done well. Slipshod methods of study or sermon preparation which may become habitual may develop. This is not fair either to the student or the church. Some students drive long distances every week and this consumes both time and energy. Some attempt too heavy an academic schedule, or too heavy a field-work program, or both, with a drain on energy and health.

The only answer to the above problems is one of scheduling of time. The student's academic load must be correlated with his field-work responsibilities in terms of the student's abilities. Some students can carry more academic hours (and maintain a student pastorate) than other students can. It is generally agreed when a heavy field-work program is undertaken, one's academic program should be extended another year or more.

Does a student receive remuneration or academic credits for field work?

This differs with different schools and locations. Most student pastors get paid for their efforts. Some churches provide a parsonage for the student and his wife or family if he is married.

This can be a real economic factor in enabling a person to secure his training. Other positions, such as those of assistant pastors or ministers of education or directors of youth work also usually provide a salary. Some tasks that do not require much time, such as teaching a church school class or sponsoring a youth group, are done on a volunteer basis. Some schools give academic credit for such experiences; some do not.

When should a person start to preach?

There are definite differences of opinion about this. Some say the sooner the better. They point out that there is no substitute for experience and the more preaching a person does while still in school, the better. Some men preach as early as the freshman year in college.

Others feel that a person should not attempt to preach until he has had opportunity to receive some training in order to be qualified to preach. They hold the opinion that actual preaching should be deferred until after the student has had some training in speech and homiletics (the art of preaching) in order that bad habits will not be established that would need to be broken or changed later. This would mean that actual preaching would be deferred until the first or second year of seminary.

What is meant by an "intern year"?

This is a year spent in a local church under the supervision of an experienced pastor. It is an attempt to provide an opportunity for supervised experiences in an actual situation before a student accepts responsibility for his own church. The value obviously is closely related to the effectiveness and skills of the pastor to whom the student is assigned.

What is clinical training for the minister?

Clinical pastoral training is a method whereby theological students and ministers gain firsthand experiences in dealing with people's problems under supervision and guidance. Training centers are maintained in general hospitals, mental hospitals, penal and correctional institutions. A full-time, qualified, chaplain must be in charge of the program. He supervises the work of the student in pastoral calling and counseling. The entire staff of physicians, psychiatrists, psychologists, and social workers shares in the instruction and casework conferences. Extensive use is made of verbatim reports of actual pastoral contacts the student has had within the institution.

There are two national programs or organizations that sponsor several centers—The Council for Clinical Training, 2 East 103rd Street, New York 29, New York, and The Institute of Pastoral Care, 50 Elm Street, Springfield, Massachusetts. Their training centers are used by students from many theological schools representing a large group of denominations. Some schools maintain their own training centers. The length of time for such training varies. The Council for Clinical Training offers a twelve-week course, although a student may take an entire clinical year if he wishes. The Institute of Pastoral Care has a six-week program. Such training is usually given credit toward a degree in the seminary.

Should one go to seminary if he is not sure that he wants to be a minister?

When a person is uncertain, he would do well to consider the matter carefully and prayerfully and to discuss it with his pastor, or perhaps with someone at the seminary. It might be that he would want to avail himself of some psychological testing or consult his denominational recruitment and guidance program.

This does not mean that a person should not go to seminary. Many people in seminary are still uncertain about what they want to do. The seminary experience itself will help a person to decide just what he wants to do. Even though he might decide later that he prefers to do something else, he should be a better-informed layman as a result of his seminary training.

The Rockefeller Theological Scholarships, described below, offer a unique opportunity for such persons.

Can a person change his mind after having started seminary?

Yes, this happens frequently. As a result of seminary experience, one may feel that he is not fitted for the ministry, or feel more qualified in some other field of service. When this is the case, it is perhaps better to make a change then than to continue in a field where he does not feel qualified or committed. This does not alter his original commitment to a life of service, or of service to and through the church. Even though he enters some other vocation, he can still live a life of service and render a service to the church as a layman.

What is the Rockefeller theological fellowship program?

This is a program established by the Rockefeller Foundation which provides 60 one-year all-expense fellowships in theological education for students who are studying in other fields but who are willing to consider the ministry. Its purpose is stated as follows:

"This program is designed for those who are not already committed to the ministry. It is intended for students who are uncertain in regard to their vocation, young persons preparing for careers in other fields, and recent graduates presently in other occupations or in the military services, who are interested in giving serious consideration to the possibility of entering the ministry. It is not a general theological fellowship program but one designed for a particular purpose, namely to discover and develop new talent for the Christian ministry."

The program is administered under the direction of the American Association of Theological Schools, 163 Nassau Street, Princeton, New Jersey.

Is it true that theological education is in a state of transition today?

Yes. In one sense it always has been and perhaps always should be. Rapid cultural changes in society, the development of the social and psychological sciences, the breaking down of denominational lines and a growing awareness of the ecumenical church are all causing theological schools to rethink their curriculum, methods, and procedures. Seminaries are more than ever aware of their responsibility and are striving to improve their procedures to do as thorough a job as possible. Such times of transition are exciting and challenging times to be gaining a theological education.

What is the Interseminary Movement?

The Interseminary Movement is the ecumenical expression of the church at the seminary level. It is a movement bringing together the students and faculties of different seminaries for fellowship, study, and enrichment. It is described in a publication of the ISM as "a movement of students and faculty who believe

in Jesus Christ as Saviour and Lord, who in institutions in the
United States are training for various aspects of the Christian
ministry; who are dedicated to the ecumenical reformation,
namely, that fundamental reawakening among individuals, congregations, and confessions, which leads to the pursuit of the
full mission of the Church of Jesus Christ in the entire world,
and which seeks greater unity among Christians and churches in
this world mission."

It has members on more than 130 campuses, which are divided
into eight regions. Its national executive is a staff member of
the National Council of Churches of Christ. It maintains a close
working relationship with the United Student Christian Council, the Student Volunteer Movement, and the American Association of Theological Schools.

The address of the Interseminary Movement is 297 Fourth
Avenue, New York 10, New York.

What is the Student Volunteer Movement?

The SVM is a fellowship of students who are interested in
missions as a life career. They meet locally, regionally, and na-
tionally for programs of study, enrichment, and fellowship. The
movement includes both those who are giving consideration to
such a career and those who have already signed a declaration
card stating their intentions to serve as missionaries.

SVM is a unit of the National Council of Churches and is
related to the Commission on Higher Education. It works in co-
operation with the World Student Christian Federation and all
groups seeking to extend the world mission of the church.

The address of the national headquarters is 257 Fourth Ave.,
New York 10, New York.

How important is the library?

The importance of a library to a theological school cannot be overemphasized. This is why one of the basic requirements for accreditation in the American Association of Theological Schools is an adequate library. The knowledge of the world is contained in books. The wealth of all the ages is stored in a good library.

The library has value only as the student makes use of it. He ought not neglect such an opportunity. While he is in school, he has resources available that are not available once he gets out on the field.

There is a close correlation between the value received from classroom lectures and discussions and the use that is made of the library. It is hoped that a student will develop the habit of reading more than the minimum of the list of books that are placed on the reserve shelf. It is hoped that he will read the good books—rather the great books. He can profit from any course if he reads the best books in the field.

When a person reads, he should enter into an encounter with the author of the book. He should consider the author's point of view but not be overawed by it. He should read critically but appreciatively, make the contents of the book his own.

Should a student start his own library while in seminary?

Yes. When a person is in seminary is the time to start building his library. Inquire of the professors what are the best books in their fields, what books will last; what books will have a practical and permanent value.

A minister's library is *all-important*. His books are the tools of his trade. Dr. Trueblood has said, "A minister's library is a pitiless revelation of his mind and his usefulness." The great preachers have found time to read the great books.

Reviews in seminary bulletins and religious journals offer valuable clues as to important new books that would be worth purchasing.

Much money can be wasted on trivial and unimportant books, so select books with care. Then use them, read them, and master them.

Does the theological school provide opportunities for worship and spiritual growth?

Yes. While a seminary is basically a school, it is also a worshiping community. In regular chapel services and in special services planned for specific occasions, students and faculty alike meet in a common act of worship, devotion, and prayer. Worship practices and patterns differ with the schools and their denominational heritage and traditions, but some form of worship is a part of every school. The student will do well to make this as much a part of his seminary experience as classroom or library.

Do some students have difficulty with their own religious life while in seminary?

Yes, many do. This is inevitable. Probably everyone experiences it to some degree. The theological student is in a unique position, compared with students in other professional schools. He must study his religion and experience it at the same time. He must examine his faith and be sustained by his faith at the same time. He must consider it objectively, critically, and exactly. This can put a real strain on one's personal devotional appreciation and experience.

Some find seminary has a totally different approach to some religious matters from that the student was used to in his home church or in his college experience. His theological professor may have a different attitude toward the authority of the Scripture, or be of a different theological orientation from the student's pastor or former professor. He may find that two professors on the same faculty differ at points, yet he has courses under both professors. He not only has the problem of passing the courses, but he must think through his own faith and theological position. Some students develop quite a feeling of anxiety because of their confusion and uncertainty. Some feel a bit of guilt even to ask questions about their faith. All of this varies with different students. Some face the necessity of rethinking their whole religious position; others have no difficulty at all. It is encouraging to say that most come through the experience with a religious experience that is much stronger and more adequate.

Does a B.D. degree complete one's training for the ministry?

No, it is only the beginning. Henry Ward Beecher, addressing the students at Yale, said, "You have not begun your education yet. You are but getting ready to study when you begin to preach." We recognize the truth of what he said. It is the same idea that was expressed in the recent study of theological education when it was stated that the fundamental problem of theological training is not to train preachers and pastors, but to help men become "self-educating" so that they will continue their growth and continue to prepare themselves through the years.

In other words, a B.D. degree gives what is felt to be the basis for a man to carry on a ministry. It is fully recognized that this job is never done; his degree should give him the background so that he will continue to improve his effectiveness throughout his ministry.

Can one take theological training beyond the B.D. degree?

Yes. Many seminaries offer a Th.M. (Master of Theology); some offer a Th.D. (Doctor of Theology) and a few, a Ph.D. (Doctor of Philosophy) degree. The Master of Theology degree usually requires a minimum of 30 hours or one year above the B.D. degree. The Th.D. and Ph.D. usually require 90 hours or 3 years. For exact requirements write to the school and secure a catalog.

What is a D.D. degree?

D.D. stands for Doctor of Divinity. It is an honorary degree conferred by a college or seminary upon someone they feel has rendered an outstanding service in the religious field. It is sometimes referred to as an unearned degree. This means that it is not a degree that is earned in an academic program requiring a specified number of hours or semesters of study. In other words, it is a recognition granted by a school for significant service or achievement.

Can a man continue his education in the pastorate?

Yes, he can and should.

There are various possibilities that one can follow. An organized program of reading is essential. This means *definite, planned* reading that covers certain areas; reading the great books, the significant books, and not just the popular ones; creative reading, and critical reading. One hour of disciplined reading every day will add up to 20 to 30 books a year. Writing as well as reading is a help. This is valuable whether or not the writing is done for publication. Ideas become our own when we can express them in words and put them down on paper.

Most schools offer short summer courses, pastors' institutes, and lectureships—all of which have value. Some schools offer extension or home study courses. One such course a year for five years would be the equivalent of 15 hours' credit.

A person can do much to improve the effectiveness of his practical ministry by keeping records of his calls and counseling cases. He should go over them, evaluate them, and ask himself such questions as "What did this behavior mean? What should I have done here? How could this have been improved?" It has even greater value if he can go over such records with a psychologist, social worker, psychiatrist, family counselor, or one of the other specialists who deal with people's needs and problems. This sharing of insights and points of view does much to make a person aware of the implications of a problem and improve his own effectiveness.

Groups of ministers in a community can do much by joining in informal groups for the purpose of mutual growth and development. We do not mean the traditional ministerial association with its speaker and lunch although this has a real value. An informal group that meets to share great books, great ideas, contemporary developments in Christian thought will lead to growth and development.

CHAPTER 8

Some Practical Questions
about the Ministry

What are the working conditions in the ministry?

There are certain very practical and important questions that vocational counselors say ought to be asked about any job or any position, such as:

What are the conditions of work?
What are the hours?
Is there much overtime?
Are there any particular busy seasons? Any slack seasons?
Are there any occupational hazards?
What are the opportunities for employment?
What is the trend in employment?
What is the average income?
What is the average starting income?
What is the range of income?
What are the vacation arrangements?
What retirement plans are available?

What are the opportunities for promotion?
How are the promotions obtained?[1]

We often hesitate to ask such questions about the ministry, for fear of being misinterpreted or misunderstood. No man wants to be considered mercenary or interested primarily in the size of his salary or the length of his vacation. Nevertheless, these questions are very practical and their answers are very important.

In the main it can be said that the working conditions are very favorable. The work is both interesting and vital. There is more to a job than the work one does, or the salary he receives. It influences where one lives, how one lives, one's associates and circle of friends, one's place in the community, one's standard of living, and one's outlook on life. In all of this the minister is in a favored position.

What is the salary?

This is a very practical and realistic question. It is also difficult to answer. There probably is as wide a variation in salaries in the ministry as there is in any other profession.

There is an old saying, "No one goes into the ministry to get rich." That is true; at least we hope it is. The general implications of such a statement are that ministers are underpaid. Many of them are, but not all of them.

It is true that salaries of ministers are usually lower than those of men in other professions who have spent a similar amount of time in study and preparation. It is true that some unskilled workers, truck drivers, for example, may be making

---

[1]Humphreys and Traxler: *Guidance Service*. Chicago: Science Research Association, 1954, p. 289. Used by permission.

more money than some ministers. At the same time a minister's salary may run higher than the average for wage earners in his congregation. While ministers' salaries may not be as high as they might be, much of the complaint about ministers' salaries has been exaggerated and unfortunate. After all, the compensations come in other ways.

We can't attempt to say what ministers' salaries are because of the variation mentioned above. Some men live almost on a subsistence level, though giving full time. Some salaries (though they are the exception) are as high as $25,000 a year. In addition to a cash salary, most churches provide a parsonage or a manse, or some housing allowance. Some churches also provide utilities. There are also wedding and funeral fees, occasional commencement addresses and similar speaking opportunities that are a small added source of income. The minister does not have to provide his own office space or office equipment and, if the church has a staff, he does not have to hire his own secretary. There are other items that vary with the local church. Many churches provide such expenses as car and travel allowances, convention expense and some have a book fund for the pastor's use.

What is true of salaries in general is also true of starting salaries. We can't say what a person can expect in the way of a salary because it depends on the denomination or the area of the country, and on the ability of the person, on general economic conditions, and on the opportunities that may present themselves. A young person wishing more definite information would do well to consult his local area or district representative.

What are the hours?

Questions about hours, workweek, and overtime simply do not apply to the ministry. This is one of the problems. The minister punches no time clock. There is no such thing as an eight-hour day or a five-day week. He often works ten, twelve, or more hours a day and very commonly works seven days a week.

The ministry is conceived as a task to be done, a service rendered and cannot be evaluated in terms of hours spent.

What are vacation arrangements?

Like salaries, this varies. It would range from one week to three months, with a month probably the average. This would be more generous than is available to most members of a congregation.

Does the church provide housing?

The majority of churches do. It is the custom in Protestantism for the church to provide a parsonage or manse for the minister and his family. This is not listed as salary and therefore not subject to income tax. Where housing is not provided, there is usually a monthly housing allowance which the minister can apply as rent or payments on a house of his own.

Is the minister eligible for social security?

Yes. By a recent act of Congress, the minister is eligible for social security benefits as a self-employed person. He pays his own assessments on a percentage basis. It cannot be done by the church. This entitles him to the same considerations as anyone else who is covered by the Social Security Act. Once he has entered social security, he cannot withdraw. Many ministers take advantage of this opportunity to provide more retirement and old-age protection. For full information write your national office or contact your local social security office.

What retirement plans are provided?

This varies with the denomination and the local church. Most denominations now have a retirement program. In some groups it is optional whether or not the minister or the local church participates. It is becoming increasingly accepted as a regular and necessary part of a church's obligation to the ministry. The usual arrangement is for the minister to pay a percentage of his salary and the church to pay a percentage to a pension fund that makes available a source of income when the minister reaches retirement age.

Retirement age usually is listed as sixty-five or seventy years, but this varies with the groups.

A letter to the national office of any denomination would secure the information regarding that group's retirement plan.

Does a minister have to pay income tax?

It is strange that such a question should be asked, but some people do have the mistaken idea that he is exempt from income tax. The answer is that the minister pays an income tax the same as anyone else.

What are the opportunities for employment?

Anyone making extensive preparation for a vocation wants to have some assurance that there will be opportunity for employ-

ment or service when his preparation is completed. In vocational guidance one of the basic questions that is asked of any
field of work is: What is the labor market? Is the vocation
overcrowded? What are the trends in employment?

Here the minister is in an enviable position. Because of the
great shortage of ministers, there are many positions open and
all indications are that this will be true for some time to come.
We have discussed the reasons for the shortage elsewhere. A recent publication of the National Council of Churches of Christ
in America estimated that Protestant churches in America are at
least 25,000 short of the number of ministers required to fill
their churches and in the next 20 years 600,000 new ministers
will be required to meet even normal needs of replacement and
responsibility.[1] The implications of such a situation are obvious.

If I become a minister, do I have to start in some poor, strug-
gling church?

There is no common answer to this. Not many men start at
the top in any profession. Many ministers begin in churches
that have very adequate facilities, a good attendance, and a spirit
of faith and service. Others do have what might be termed
more difficult assignments or, as the question states it, a "poor,
struggling church."

Certain things should be pointed out. It is an advantage to
begin where the program is small and the responsibilities are not
too heavy. Such a program is not unimportant. In this regard
there are no small churches. The people in these churches need
a ministry just as much as the people in a large church where
the minister receives a large salary. They may need it even

---

[1]See "National Council Outlook," "The Ministerial Crisis," May, 1957, p. 11.

more than those in a large church. If the minister sees this church as a challenge, as an opportunity to render a service, and to meet a need, his ministry takes on a new perspective. Many a man has testified that his years in a so-called "small struggling church" were among the most pleasant and fruitful years of his ministry.

Isn't there a great deal of difference between churches?

Yes. While the gospel is the same and the basic needs of people are essentially the same, there is a great deal of difference in the program and activities, in the attitudes of people in a small rural church in the Midwest and a large city church in downtown New York or Cleveland.

Churches, like people, have personalities. They are influenced by their surroundings. There are downtown churches, churches on or near a campus, and suburban or neighborhood churches in new housing areas. There are churches in small towns and villages, and often in the open country.

Some seminaries offer specialized courses in the urban or the rural church. While a minister can't always decide where he will serve, he would do well to think through the group that he understands the best and the type of church that he would prefer to serve.

What is a minister's or a theological student's draft classification?

Section 162243 of the Selective Service Regulations, dated September 28, 1951, provides for a IV-D, or deferred classification for all ministers of religion or theological students who are pursuing a full-time course of instruction in a duly recognized theological or divinity school.

If a student is still in college or even in high school and wishes to secure this deferred status, he should observe the following procedures:

(1) Sign a statement of purpose or life commitment card, or whatever device is provided by his own denomination and see that this statement is on file in the national headquarters of his own communion.

(2) Send a written endorsement from his own pastor and the official body of his local church to his national office and to the local draft board.

(3) Secure a statement from the school he is now attending certifying the fact that he is pursuing a full course leading to theological training. Send a copy of this statement to the local draft board.

(4) Make application to a recognized theological school for pre-enrollment to be admitted upon satisfactory completion of college studies. Secure a statement of acceptance as a pre-theological student from the seminary and send a copy, with the other letters mentioned above, to the draft board and his own national office.

(5) Keep a carbon of each of these letters for his own personal file.

Are there opportunities for women in the ministry?

If this question means, "Are there opportunities for women in the church vocations?" the answer is, "Yes, there are many." If the question means, "Are there opportunities for women in the preaching ministry?" the answer is, "They are very limited."

Some denominations do not ordain any women to the preaching ministry; some do, but the number who become pastors of churches is relatively small.

There are many opportunities for women in such fields as religious education, missions, and church social work. Religious education includes a wide variety of responsibilities. Some religious educators are in local churches. Some serve on state and national staffs. Some specialize in various age levels, such as children's work or youth work. Missions, of course, is a wide field with a great variety of services.

Can an older person enter the ministry?

One answer to this question is that many of them do. Some men who have been in the business or professional world for a number of years feel the call to the ministry, leave their occupations, and go back to school to prepare themselves for the ministry. Some men in the armed services have felt as a result of their experiences that they would like to enter the field of Christian service and they, too, on leaving the service, prepare themselves for one of the church vocations.

Each case must be seen in its own light. Whether or not an individual should give up a career to return to school and all that it entails must be determined in the light of many factors. Such a person must evaluate his own motivations, his own qualifications and opportunities, the attitudes of his family, and everything else related to the decision.

For our purpose, it is sufficient to say that if these things (such as motivation, qualification, etc.) are favorable, there is no reason why such a program cannot be accomplished; in fact, a man's maturity of outlook, his experiences in the business and professional world may give him some definite advantages.

Does one have to announce publicly that he is going to enter the ministry?

Different churches have different customs at this point. Some have a public service of recognition prior to ordination; some do not. The important thing is the sense of commitment and dedication a person feels within himself.

To whom should one make his commitment?

Different churches have different practices. In some groups a statement is made to the local church; in some to a state commission on the ministry; in others to a superintendent, bishop, or some other official. A letter addressed to the national office of a person's own denomination will reach the right person and secure the necessary information.

It is advisable to have accurate information as to procedure in order to avoid problems about ordination, selective service, and such matters.

What is meant by "ordination" to the ministry?

The word ordain means to appoint, or to "invest with authority." When one is ordained into the ministry, he is formally accepted and commissioned by the church to serve as a minister of the gospel. Ordination usually comes at the completion of one's training although some men are ordained while still in seminary.

There is a wide diversity of practice as to qualification for ordination, as to who determines candidates for ordination and who conducts the service of ordination. With some groups it is only the ecclesiastical body that can ordain. In other communions, the local church has the authority to ordain.

For full information as to the practices of any particular denomination, inquire of a local pastor or contact the state or national office.

What does it mean to be licensed to preach?

Different churches have different practices, but the majority have a licensing procedure which enables a theological student, or perhaps a layman who may be supplying a church, to carry on certain ministerial duties, such as conducting baptisms, officiating at weddings and funerals, while serving as the pastor of the church.

It is not full ordination but enables a man to continue to serve a church. Different denominations have different practices as to who can license a man to preach and who is qualified to receive such a license.

What is the time limit on a license or ordination?

License is usually for one year, but renewable. Ordination is ordinarily for life.

CHAPTER 9

The
Satisfactions and Discouragements
of the
Ministry

What are the satisfactions of the ministry?

The first and most important is the satisfaction that comes from knowing one is giving himself to something that is of concern to God himself. Life has no greater challenge, privilege, or responsibility.

Someone has said that one of life's greatest values is to be needed and to feel that with God's help you can meet that need. That is one of the satisfactions of the ministry—one knows he is investing himself in a great cause and serving a great need.

There is the very great satisfaction that comes from helping people. The minister has the high privilege of working with people, helping them in times of need, watching them grow and develop in the Christian life and in Christian understanding. He has the great satisfaction of knowing that he has made some small contribution to their lives.

A book on vocational guidance says that one question that should be asked of any vocation is, "What are the possibilities for personal growth?" There is probably no walk of life that offers more opportunities for personal growth—socially, educationally, spiritually—than the ministry.

There are many other things that could be listed. The minister has fine associations, rich friendships within his congregation, within his community, and with others in the ministry. He has pleasant surroundings and a place of prestige and responsibility in the community. The list is endless. The greatest satisfactions are intangible.

Jesus said the first two commandments were to love God with all one's heart, mind, soul and strength, and to love one's neighbor as oneself. This applies to all men, but the minister has the high privilege of applying such teachings through his life and his vocation.

What are the discouragements of the ministry?

The discouragements of the ministry will be different with different people. What is highly satisfying to one may not be to another. What is discouraging to one may be a source of satisfaction to another; for example, some get a great deal of pleasure from fund raising, for others it is very difficult. Some find writing and study very satisfying. Other find it drudgery and highly monotonous. Some problems vary in degree. Some opposition may be challenging and stimulating; too much opposition may be discouraging and defeating.

The indifference of people is another discouragement. A minister usually has high ideals and lofty ambitions for the church and its program. The people in the church may not share his enthusiasm. They may not welcome his new ideas or share some

38695

of his views. This is often difficult for a minister to accept. He sees his visions and dreams frustrated and destroyed because people will not accept responsibility or are negligent or ineffective in their tasks. The pastor will see great plans thwarted because people will give more time to their clubs and lodges than to the church; he will see great possibilities unrealized because people spend more on pleasure than they will invest in the cause of Christ and his church.

The church is made up of people, very human people, with all of the limitations and failings of human nature. Quarreling, bitterness, jealousy, pride, and narrowness often enter into church activities as well as into other areas of life.

Open opposition may present itself. Anyone who stands for the right and opposes evil may well expect some opposition. All new ideas and forward-looking movements have met with opposition.

Church work is slow. Some of the results of a man's efforts may not be evident for many years. At times it may seem as though he is making no progress.

Many ministers find it difficult to watch men in other professions attain financial success and social prestige beyond anything they have realized.

There are other problems that could be listed. Suffice it to say that it should be recognized that the ministry is a difficult task. It does have its moments of discouragement and seeming defeat.

Does the work of the ministry become monotonous?

Actually, the work of the ministry is probably as varied and as creative as that of any in society. The minister has an infinite variety of tasks. He serves as preacher, teacher, counselor, a bit of a social worker, something of a psychologist, an administrator,

Lincoln Christian College

an organizer, reformer, community servant, leader in worship, a scholar—for some this becomes a problem; it seems to be more than one man can do—but he never should be bored.

There is a real opportunity to be creative in a variety of ways. For some this will come through preaching; for others through scholarship; for some through administration; for others through social service or community activities, but the opportunities are there.

Does a minister have any time of his own?

Time is one of the minister's very real problems. There are so many demands made upon him that time for his family, time for relaxation, and time for personal growth often get crowded out.

One pulpit committee in a church looking for a new minister decided that they would list the things they wanted him to do each week and the time it would take to do them. Each member made a separate list. They included such things as preaching, calling on the sick, conducting weddings, meeting with boards and committees, working with youth groups and choirs, counseling, officiating at funerals, consulting with church officials, correspondence and phone calls, attending denominational and interdenominational gatherings, preparing the church bulletin and newsletter, calling on prospects, appearing at social engagements and receptions, keeping church records, writing articles, preparing sermons, personal study, meditation, preparation of talks for service clubs, school assemblies, and so forth.

When they had completed their lists, they found that all these services would take over 300 hours a week.

This is an obvious exaggeration, but it points out the problem. The result is that a minister's family may be neglected. He may not obtain sufficient rest and relaxation and some of the more important things may be crowded out by trivial details.

What is the solution to the problem of time?

Each person must find a solution that fits his own situation. Part of the problem is lack of organization. A minister needs to organize his time, work out a schedule, and stick to it. Here people differ. Just as some do not like to operate their finances on a budget, some prefer not to operate on a time budget, but some means of evaluating and controlling one's time is necessary.

A minister needs to establish certain priorities. A pastor of a medium-sized church said, "I have to go to so many committee meetings and do so much organization work I don't have time to pray." A man who is that busy is too busy. Some things must never be crowded out.

A minister needs to preserve and safeguard some time for his family. He needs to have some time to relax and enjoy himself. He will do better work if he does. He needs to save time to study, to think, and to grow. He needs time for personal meditation, worship, and prayer. Such time well spent will make the time spent on other activities more effective.

Is a minister's family subject to constant scrutiny and criticism?

A minister and his family do live in the public eye, so to speak. They are expected to be an example. Their faults are the subject of general discussion. This can be a problem. However, it can be said that the tendency to be overly critical of the minister and his family is rapidly decreasing. He has no greater problem than anyone else does who is in public life.

There is another side that should be mentioned. The minister's family, because of his position in the community, has opportunity, recognition, and consideration that more than compensate for any public scrutiny.

CHAPTER 10

The Minister's Attitudes and Personal Religious Life

Which is more important: methods and techniques or the person who uses them?

There is an old Chinese proverb which says, "A good method used by a bad person will produce bad results, but a bad method used by a good person will produce good results." That is not always true but there is truth in it.

The value of methods and techniques is recognized by all. Though a man may have the best of intentions, he may not achieve many results if he has not learned the right skills and methods. One of the primary tasks a person must accomplish in seminary is to master all the necessary techniques of preaching, counseling, and church administration. If a student does not accomplish this task, he will weaken the effectiveness of his ministry. It is only fair to recognize, however, that methods cannot be separated from the man who uses them.

What a man is is sometimes more important than what he does. A minister's effectiveness in leading a church depends as much on his understanding of the people as it does on an understanding of the techniques of administration. His effectiveness in preaching will depend on his character and personality as much as it will on his skill in sermon construction and public speaking. His pastoral work will be determined just as much by his attitudes and his relationship with people as it will on counseling techniques and procedures.

What attitudes are important for the ministry?

Any listing of separate attitudes is artificial and misleading. It is a man's total personality that counts. Nevertheless, for purposes of discussion, there are certain things we would mention.

Humility. Jesus said, "Everyone who exalts himself will be humbled, and he who humbles himself will be exalted." Someone has said that a minister's two greatest temptations are laziness and pride. He is the recipient of much praise. He is in a position of recognition and prestige. It is easy to lose his humility and thus his influence.

Friendliness. Washington Gladden used to say that the minister ought to be the one man in the community to whom anyone in need of a friend would feel free to turn. Christianity began as a friendship. The minister must be a friend to his people, to all people.

Understanding. It is not only friendship that is needed, but understanding. Ian MacLaren, out of a long ministry, used to say, "Be kind; everyone you meet is fighting a hard battle." He understood. Understanding is the ability to put oneself in the place of another.

Industry. It is not without reason that laziness was listed with pride as the two great temptations of the ministry. There is no great achievement without great effort.

Courage. It goes without saying that a minister must have courage. He is a prophet as well as a pastor. He who stands in the line of the prophets must confront people with the reality of

God and with their own moral responsibility. He must oppose that which is evil and defend that which is good. He must be a friend of everyone but afraid of no one. He must cater to no man because of his wealth, position, or prestige. All of this takes courage.

Persistence. Many times the test of a man's ministry is not his brilliance but his patience, not his eloquence but his persistence.

Anyone can serve when things are going well, when others pat him on the back and praise his efforts. Anyone can continue when results are evident and encouraging. The test comes when they are not.

When Judson went to Burma it was with the high hope of opening that continent to Christ. He worked seven years before he got one convert, seven years with no evidence of results. That is persistence.

Even the Apostle Paul was aware of this problem. Twice in his letters he urged the people to "be not weary in well doing. . . ." Perhaps he knew the meaning of this problem, too.

Faith. Everyone recognizes that the minister must have faith. Talking about faith from the pulpit is not enough. He must have an attitude of trust and commitment that permeates all his life.

No one has all of these attitudes, but all can grow in these directions. It is a gradual process. It is a lifetime task. Every minister, whether a seminarian in training or a man on the field, should discipline his attitudes of mind and spirit until they are brought more and more under the influence of Christ.

Are some temptations peculiar to the ministry?

The word "peculiar" is the difficult one. The minister does not have any temptations that no one else has. However, some of them may be accentuated by his position.

Pride. The minister is in a favored position. People look up to him; they pay him respect because of his office. He must be careful not to magnify his own importance.

Egocentricity. It is easy for the minister to think the church revolves around him and thus to become self-centered. People often pamper the minister or give him preferential treatment. The minister must constantly keep before himself a vision of "self-forgetful" service.

Self-pity. Religious work is difficult. Results are sometimes slow. It is easy to feel sorry for oneself, to slacken one's efforts, to be tempted to quit.

Competition. This refers primarily to competition with other ministers. We live in a competitive society. It is present in the business world, the sports world, and almost everywhere we turn. It is also present in the church. There is competition between churches for new members, competition between pastors for positions, honors, and recognitions. Such elements are always present, but a minister's Christian spirit must always control the spirit of competition.

Indolence. A minister is his own boss; he keeps no hours except the ones he regulates for himself. It is easy to deceive himself into thinking he is busy wasting time, or that he is overworked when he is not. It takes real discipline to overcome the temptation to fritter away time.

Resentment, jealousy, bitterness. It might seem that these need not to be mentioned, that the minister should live by the law of love. It is true that he should. He, too, has experiences when his plans are frustrated, his motives questioned, his program opposed. Then it is a test of a man's soul whether he can rise above the temptation to give in to the common attitudes of resentment and bitterness and meet these situations in the spirit of love.

What is the secret of a minister's influence?

When George Buttrick was pastor of Madison Avenue Presbyterian Church in New York City, the church had several seminary students who did "field work" in the church each year. At one of the regular seminars that were held with the group, they discussed the secret of a minister's influence. They considered many matters that contribute to a minister's influence—appearance, intellectual ability, character. All these things played a part. The one thing they felt outweighed all others was the purity of a man's motives.[1]

Nothing will destroy a man's ministry more quickly than a question about his sincerity. Morley said of Gladstone, "We believe in no man's infallibility but it is restful to believe in one man's integrity." No congregation should ever have occasion to doubt their minister's integrity.

What is a common characteristic of the great preachers?

Concern about their people is a universal characteristic. A visitor to Phillips Brooks' services said the thing that impressed him about Brooks's preaching was his obvious love for his congregation.

When John Frederic Oberlin was carrying on an effective ministry in the Vosges Mountains of France, he used to spend an hour a day in prayer for his people. During this hour he mentioned them one by one, by name. His people knew this and passed his house in silence because they knew their pastor was praying for them. He was that much concerned.

All great pastors have had a great concern.

---

[1] cf. Buttrick, Jesus Came Preaching, Scribners, 1936, p. 170.

How can a minister maintain attitudes of good will and love when so many people are unlovely?

The first thing we would say is that Jesus did it. When we read the stories in the Gospels, we should realize that these were real people Jesus dealt with—dishonest tax collectors, hardened sinners, women of the streets. Even his closest followers often misunderstood him, and frequently disappointed him. One of them denied him; another betrayed him. The very people he desired to serve forsook him and opposed him—but he never diminished his efforts or doubted that they were worth while. On the very cross he prayed for those who put him there.

The minister, too, deals with real people—all kinds of people, good, bad, and indifferent. Of course, he will like some more than others. While he can only approach from afar the sacrificial, forgiving, all-inclusive love that was shown by Jesus, he can move in this direction. The minister can recognize that people's very mistakes, their shortcomings, their sins are symptoms of a need. While he continues to hate the sin, he must love the sinner. He will recognize that their very unacceptable behavior is evidence of a need that it is his place to serve.

If a minister pauses to take a long look at his own life, he will be less critical of others. A consciousness of his own mistakes and shortcomings should make him more understanding of others.

How can one become a minister when the church has so many weaknesses and is so full of hypocrites?

This question has been variously stated in a number of ways. It is a real problem. The church does have many weaknesses: it is tragically divided, often weak and ineffective and at times seems to be making little impression in the world. Some things should be pointed out however. With all of its weaknesses, it is still the oldest institution in society, except for the synagogue from which it came. No government or other institution has lasted as long. It has survived persecutions, wars, ridicule, opposition, and everything else, but it continues to go on. It has produced the best in our life and culture. It was the founder of schools and hospitals. It was the background from which came modern social service, political reforms, and even democracy itself.

As for the people in the church, of course they have weaknesses, for the church is made up of people with all of their imperfections.

Of course the church has weaknesses, and people in the church make mistakes—some may even be hypocrites. This is the very reason ministers are needed.

It should also be said that the church includes good people, too. Down through the centuries the church has done more to create lives of sincere Christian character than all other institutions put together. Such people are in the church today.

How important is a minister's personal religious life?

The personal religious life of a minister or theological student is the heart or the foundation of his religious experience and it is a point at which many express problems or dissatisfaction.

Time itself can be a problem. The minister and theological student both find their days crowded with so many activities and responsibilities that it is difficult to find a time of uninterrupted quiet, some period of silence and solitude when they can cultivate and nurture their spiritual experience.

It is further complicated by the fact that the minister is professionally engaged in religious activities. It is not enough to assume that because he directs a religious program or speaks on religious subjects, all his own religious needs are being met. He may let the "speaking about" spiritual things become a substitute for doing them.

Theological students also have a problem. There is a difference in studying religion and being religious. The theological student must study and analyze his faith and live by it at the same time. That is not easy. Many express concern at this point. Some feel guilty because their own religious life is not as vital or as real as they think that it should be.

A personal religious life is important for the minister for the same reason that it is important for everyone else. He needs a consciousness of the presence of God in his daily life. He needs the assurance of forgiveness and renewal. He needs a source of courage and strength. He needs guidance and understanding so that he sees life from a divine perspective. He needs inspiration; he needs to be challenged to live up to his best; he needs to be sustained in moments of discouragement and disappointment. He needs to have his purposes clarified, his ambitions purified, his ideals strengthened, and his hopes renewed. He needs to see others with the understanding that comes from love and a spirit of prayer. All these things are found through his personal religious life.

What are the resources for a personal religious life?

They are the same for the theological student as they are for everyone else—prayer, scripture, public worship, inspirational and devotional literature, moments of silence, and periods of solitude and meditation. These are the "means of grace" that have strengthened and enriched men's lives from the days before history was recorded until the present time.

What are the methods or the principles that should govern a minister's personal devotional life?

No one can tell another how he should pray or how he should observe his own private religious life. Each man must find his own methods. What is real to one may not be to another. Dick Sheppard used to arise at dawn and look out over the city of London. As he meditated on the needs of the people, he made this a time of prayer. Muriel Lester says she can pray quite effectively while walking briskly down the street. One pastor in New York says that riding the subway becomes for him a moment of meditation and devotion. Some prefer to go to the sanctuary of a church and there, looking at the altar or perhaps a cross, they find themselves in the mood of prayer. Perhaps the majority prefer to remain in their own room, following the instructions of the passage in the Sermon on the Mount which says, "But when you pray, go into your room and shut the door and pray to your Father who is in secret; and your Father who sees in secret will reward you." (Matthew 6:6.)

Each man must find the method or the plan that is real to him—but there must be some plan. Unless there is some plan, prayer will be neglected or crowded out. The plan may change from time to time; in fact, it probably should change as one's experience changes and grows, but some plan must be preserved. It must be regular. "We do well the things we do often." It must be sincere.

Developing a devotional life takes time—not just days or weeks, but years. In fact, it takes a lifetime. Brother Lawrence wrote a little book called *The Practice of the Presence of God* which is recognized as one of the classics of the devotional life. Yet he said that he spent ten years before he had any real sense of reality in prayer.

APPENDIX I

On Learning How to Study

What makes for academic success in college and seminary?

Academic success is dependent upon three things. (1) *Ability*. A certain amount of intellectual ability is necessary if one is to achieve success in college. Academic achievement requires above-average ability. (2) *Motivation*. Ability alone is not enough. Some who have the ability do not succeed in college. Some do not even make the effort. Success in college, or any place else for that matter, depends on motivation. It is motivation that is determined by a person's interests, ambitions, and desires. It is motivation that determines how hard a person will try, whether he will persist, and whether he will be thorough and complete. (3) *Study Habits*. In addition to ability and motivation, a person needs to develop certain practices and skills in order that his work will be effective. One might compare it to learning to play tennis. A person may have the native ability and the motivation or desire, but it is through learning certain skills and techniques that he actually learns to play. He develops techniques so that his desires become a reality. The person who would achieve academic success also needs to develop certain skills and techniques. Only as he does so can he utilize his abilities to the fullest extent.

Can a person actually improve his study habits and thus improve his understanding and his grades?

Definitely yes. Psychologists and educators have discovered by extensive research that there are some definite principles and rules of study that work. One might almost say there is a science of study. Schools don't often teach these methods; they assume that a student will stumble onto them. Every student would do well to study the art of "how to study."

Does it make any difference where or when a person studies?

Yes. Both the time and place a person studies are important. The "mind set" has much to do with the ability to concentrate and get quickly into a task. Most authorities in the field advocate having a regular time and a regular place to study.

How important are the physical surroundings of study?

They are not the main consideration, but they are obviously important. Poor ventilation and inadequate light can limit the value of an evening of study; good light and good ventilation are an aid to study. Even the chair one uses is important. The story is told of a student who would get his text, notebook, and pencil, settle comfortably in an easy chair, and go to sleep. One shouldn't be too comfortable. A straight chair at a table or desk is a better study chair than a davenport or overstuffed chair.

What can a person do about distractions?

Avoid them, first of all. Select a time and place that is as free from noise interruptions and other disturbances as possible.

Don't be too disturbed when they occur, as they will in spite of all precautions. One can accustom himself to studying under some adverse circumstances. Some studies show that concentration may even be superior if there are some minor distractions that force the student to pay attention to the task.

Is it advisable to study on a time schedule?

Scheduling time is like budgeting money. Some like it, and some don't. Experience shows that those who schedule their time usually do better work.

This is simply a matter of evaluating and organizing one's time. There is keen competition for time at both the college and seminary level. A time schedule or a time budget is an attempt to put first things first. If academic achievement is a major objective, it must be given top priority on the list. Other things must be scheduled around the time for study.

When a person makes an hour-by-hour, day-by-day, week-by-week evaluation of his time, it is often surprising how much time is available.

How rigid should a plan or schedule be?

The value of a program is directly related to the amount of persistence with which it is followed. Self-discipline is one requirement of anyone who desires to be a student.

However there will be times when it is necessary to vary the program. This doesn't mean that studying can't be done. A schedule is made to help one utilize time and do effective studying. It doesn't mean that this is the only way.

One should constantly re-evaluate his schedule and program. He should not continue in a program that is not satisfactory. He should improve the program with experience; he should change it if need be—but he should keep some plan and an objective.

Should a person study for long periods or for short ones?

Much depends upon the circumstances, but when it is possible, one should distribute study periods. Five half-hour sessions distributed through the week are far superior to one two-hour and a half session, though the actual time is the same.

Learning takes place between study sessions as well as during actual periods of concentration. The unconscious mind will organize and assimilate. A person does well to recognize and utilize this fact.

Sometimes long periods of study are necessary. When this is so, one should take occasional short breaks. The person who studies continuously for an hour or an hour and a half will accomplish more in the next hour if he takes a ten-minute break to relax, rest his eyes, and stretch his muscles before he returns to concentration again.

Should a schedule of time include items other than study and work?

Yes, it should also include time for rest, recreation, and worship. These also influence grades and academic achievement.

When they are neglected or ignored, one's total program will be affected.

Whether or not one schedules such items by days and hours is not the main consideration. The significant thing is that their importance is recognized and they are included in one's activities.

What is the best time to study for a particular lesson?

When it is possible, the best time to study is just before and just after a class. Review just before a class meets makes classroom discussion more meaningful. Studies in educational psychology point out that 40% to 50% of new material is forgotten within the first hour or two after it has been learned. Review or study right after class helps to retain this material.

How much time should a person spend on an assignment?

This depends both upon the person and the assignment. Some subjects require more time than others, considering a student's background. Some students require more time than others depending on their ability and familiarity with the subject. Generally speaking, it is felt that two hours should be set aside for study and research for every hour of classroom attendance.

Do study habits established in school carry over into one's ministry?

Yes. This is more than a matter of getting good grades, although there is little doubt that many students could improve their grades by developing better methods of study. The minister will always be a student. Good study habits developed in school will help him be a good one.

Does it make any difference how a person writes his reports and papers?

Definitely yes. Professors are only human and a good paper neatly written and correctly punctuated will usually get a better grade than a paper of equal content improperly done.

Get a good thesis guide and use it. Learn to punctuate and paragraph properly, to outline, to make proper footnotes and to list a bibliography. This will have many values beyond your uses in school.

How can I get the most from a course? How can I master a course or area of study?

This is the objective of every course. In some courses it is absolutely essential. These are a few practical suggestions.

(1) Keep abreast of the course if at all possible. Do the assigned reading as you go along. Don't leave it for the last week of the semester or the night before it must be turned in.

(2) Clear up all points that are not clear. If you are confused or uncertain about matters in the course, go to the professor and get help. Most professors are understanding and will be glad to help.

(3) Be sure you understand the vocabulary of a course. Certain areas like theology, psychology, and sociology have their own specialized vocabulary. A text or lecture can be almost unintelligible unless you understand the terms that are being used.

(4) Organize your material so you can see the course in its totality. Relate the class notes, the text if there is one, and the outside reading and assignments to each other.

(5) Include frequent well-spaced reviews to maintain thor-

ough familiarity with the material. Frequent reviews, even though quite brief, can be very effective.

(6) Study and review with others. There is value in discussion. There is value not only in getting another's point of view, but in expressing one's own views. Nothing becomes real or permanently one's own until he can verbalize it. In trying to make a point clear to others, you gain a better understanding yourselves.

(7) Overlearn for mastery. This is a term used by the educational psychologists. Briefly stated it means learning beyond that which is necessary for immediate recall, such as to pass an examination.

Many students are satisfied when they can perform adequately to meet some course requirement. The real student goes beyond these minimum requirements. He gains a thorough knowledge of the subject. He will be much more likely to remember the material after some time has elapsed. He will be able to utilize it in his later career.

This requires constant review and evaluation. It necessitates extra time and effort, reading all around a subject, and getting different points of view as well as that of the text or the required reading.

(8) Learn to prepare for examinations. The best preparation for an examination is the constant reviews mentioned above. Cramming or concentrated review and study just before an examination are helpful provided one has been studying throughout the semester. Here again study with someone else can be effective.

Try to anticipate the examination by forming questions yourself in preparation. Even though they are not the same questions, this practice will help.

In taking the examination be sure that you understand the instructions, relax, and work steadily and confidently.

Can a person learn to read more rapidly?

Yes, most people can and should. The ability to read rapidly and with understanding is one of the most important skills needed for success in college and seminary. Some would say that it is the most important. It is also highly significant for one's total ministry.

The encouraging thing is that it can be done. Much research has been done in this area. One of the definite findings is that almost everyone can increase his rate of reading. Some people have tripled their reading speed. It should be pointed out that this does not decrease comprehension, but often increases it.

Many colleges and universities have remedial reading courses and clinics for those with particular difficulties. Helpful books on the subject can be found in almost any college library.

Much can be done to increase speed of reading by those who do not have any serious problem but who wish to improve their effectiveness as students. It requires (1) persistent effort and (2) a knowledge of the techniques that are required.

Drs. Wrenn and Cole who have studied the subject extensively say that slow reading is usually caused by one of three things: (1) The person tries to read every word instead of reading by phrases or sentences. (2) He uses too many fixations, or in other words, his eyes pause too often or he follows a line across the page. (3) He says the words to himself.[1] This is called inner speech. It consists of moving the lips, tongue, and throat muscles as one reads. This is not only unnecessary but slows the rate and limits the comprehension. The eyes can read several times faster than the vocal chords can pronounce the words.

Much can be done simply by self-discipline and practice. Set up a schedule and practice reading rapidly. Learn to read by phrases. Put the fingers on the lips to avoid inner speech. Keep

[1]See Wrenn and Cole, *Reading Rapidly and Well.*

a record of the number of words you can read for a 10- or 20-minute period. Watch it over a period of days or weeks and surprising results may be obtained.

Can a person increase his comprehension in reading?

Yes. Certain principles should be followed.

(1) Read with a purpose. All reading that is effective is purposeful reading. See the value, the significance of the book you are reading for your course and in your career.

(2) Secure the author's over-all point of view and the plan of the book before you start to read. Study the table of contents, the introduction, the sub-heading, and the summary or conclusion if such is available. Then, with this perspective in mind, begin to read.

(3) Read with a pencil in hand. Underline sentences that you want to remember, make notes in the margin (if you own the book), and then you have a basis for quick and effective review.

(4) Read creatively. Ask questions. Be constructively critical. What were its weaknesses? What were its strength and values? How would the author's position compare with others who have written in the same general field or area? Recite as you read. Ask yourself how you would prepare an examination on this material.

(5) Learn to skim a book. Some books are only worth skimming. With some books we can get the author's point of view by this method and this is all that is desired or necessary. This leaves time to read something else.

Many books cover the same material or the same area. There is no value in continuous duplication. A rapid reading for the author's point of view is an aid to overlearning.

Some books cannot and should not be merely glanced at. A technical book, a book in an area new to you, or a basic or profound book should be read carefully and thoroughly.

(6) Review your reading. After having read the book, check back over the sentences that you have underlined and the notes that you have taken. Reread portions that seemed of real value or that were not clear. By reviewing you make the material your own; you often find values that were missed on the first reading.

What are proper mental attitudes for effective study?

(1) Study with a purpose. Recognize the importance of motivation. Many a person has the ability to master a field but lacks the motivation that challenges him to do it.

For this reason a person should keep before him both immediate and long-range goals. Studying becomes alive when its practical application is apparent. During the war it was found that men studied most effectively when they could see the relationship of the material either to a promotion or to survival.

Each task has an immediate goal—the requirement of a course, the passing of an examination. It also has a long-range goal—the effectiveness of one's life of service. Both should be kept in mind.

(2) Do not wait for inspiration; strive for it. Interest often follows effort. Get at the task, begin to read, or to write, or whatever else is required—such effort will create interest.

The student must do certain work because certain requirements demand it at certain times. This is not dissimilar to the ministry which demands a sermon each week whether the minister feels particularly creative or not. In both cases the demands of the situation must provide the inspiration.

(3) Actually study when you study. It is easy to deceive one's self at this point. A person can waste time listening to the radio, daydreaming, doing everything but studying, and, because he is sitting at a desk or in the library, convince himself that he is studying. A person must use real self-discipline if he wants to be a scholar.

(4) Concentrate on the task at hand. Plan your time so you need to do only one task at a time. When this is done, lay it aside and turn to another. If something else comes to mind while you are studying, jot it down and put it aside—then go on with the task at hand.

Develop the capacity to do "do one thing at a time." The Apostle Paul gave good advice to the student when he said, "This one thing I do."

(5) Don't give in to the thought that because it is too hot, because it is late afternoon, because someone is typing down the hall, or for any other reason or excuse, you can't study. These factors are important, but experiments show that any person can study almost any time or place if he has the motivation.

(6) Be creative. Recite to yourself as you study. Criticize the material. Try to anticipate the professor. Ask youself what questions he will ask in class. Relate this material to practical experience. How will this help in your vocational plan? How can this material be used for a life of larger service?

APPENDIX II

Denominational Offices

Disciples of Christ
Office of Ministerial Services
222 South Downey Avenue
Indianapolis 7, Indiana

African Methodist Episcopal Church
Division of Educational Institutions
414 Eighth Avenue, South
Nashville 3, Tennessee

The Moravian Church in America (North),
Board of Education and Evangelism
79 West Church Street
Bethlehem, Pennsylvania

Congregational Christian Churches
(United Church of Christ)
Department of the Ministry
287 Fourth Avenue
New York 10, New York

Five Years Meeting of Friends
503 S. Main Street
New Castle, Indiana

Evangelical United Brethren Church
Commission on Ministerial Training
Knott Building
Dayton 2, Ohio

National Baptist Convention, U.S.A., Inc.
c/o Dean Allix B. James
Virginia Union University
Richmond 20, Virginia

Church of the Brethren
Director of Ministry and Evangelism
22 South State Street
Elgin, Illinois

Protestant Episcopal Church
Unit of Church Vocations
281 Fourth Avenue
New York 10, New York

American Baptist Convention
Department of Theological Education
152 Madison Avenue
New York 16, New York

Church of the Nazarene
Department of Education
6401 The Paseo
Kansas City 10, Missouri

The Methodist Church
Department of Ministerial Education
Post Office Box 871
Nashville 2, Tennessee

The Church of God
Board of Christian Education
1303 E. Fifth Street
Anderson, Indiana

The United Presbyterian Church, U.S.A.
Department of Vocation
808 Witherspoon Building
Philadelphia 7, Pennsylvania

The Presbyterian Church, U.S.
Department of Christian Vocation
8 North Sixth Street
Richmond 9, Virginia

The United Lutheran Church
Board of Higher Education
231 Madison Avenue
New York 16, New York

The Reformed Church in America
Stewardship Council
156 Fifth Avenue
New York 10, New York

African Methodist Episcopal Zion Church
38 Acqueduct Place
Yonkers, New York

Evangelical and Reformed Church
(United Church of Christ)
Commission on the Ministry
2969 West Twenty-fifth Street
Cleveland 13, Ohio

Other Offices

American Personnel and Guidance Association
1534 "O" Street, N.W.
Washington, D. C.

Young Men's Christian Association
Personnel Services
291 Broadway
New York 7, New York

American Association of Theological Schools
1250 Knott Building
Dayton 2, Ohio

AATS—Rockefeller Brothers Theological Fellowship Fund, Inc.
163 Nassau Street
Princeton, New Jersey

National Council of Churches
Department of the Ministry
257 Fourth Avenue
New York 10, New York

3 4711 00154 8132